TRENTO

Books LLC®, Reference Series, Memphis, USA, 2011. www.booksllc.net. Copyright: http://creativecommons.org/licenses/by-sa/3.0/deed.en

Table of Contents

People from Trento
Adolph Giesl-Gieslingen 1
Adriana Volpe 2
Alessandro Bonetti.......................... 2
Alessandro Vittoria 3
Andrea Pozzo 3
Andrea Stoppini 6
Antonio da Trento 6
Beniamino Andreatta 6
Bice Bones 7
Cesare Battisti (politician) 7
Cesare Maestri 8
Chiara Lubich......................... 8
Christoph Anton Migazzi................. 10
Daniel Oss........................... 11
Ernest von Koerber 12
Francesca Dallapé 13
Francesca Neri 13
Francesco Antonio Bonporti 14
Galeazzo von Thun und Hohenstein . 15
Gianna Pederzini 15
Giorgio Moser........................ 15
Giovanni Battista Ceschi a Santa
Croce 16
Giovanni Kessler..................... 16
Giulia Turco 17
Giulio Alessandrini 17
Hermann Zingerle 18
Ida Dalser 18
Jacob Acontius 19
Johann Baptist von Lampi the
Younger.............................. 20
Leonardo Bertagnolli 20
Leopold Ernst von Firmian 20
Lorenzo Bernardi 21
Lorenzo Dellai....................... 22
Ludovico Madruzzo 22
Marcello Guarducci................... 23
Margherita Cagol 23
Mariano Piccoli 23
Martino Martini 23
Matthias Gallas 26
Mauro Trentini 26
Mirko Bortolotti 26
Paolo Oss Mazzurana......................... 27
Renzo Cramerotti.............................. 28
Roberto Sighel.................................. 28
Rody Mirri....................................... 29

Trento
Cognola.. 29
Mattarello.. 30
Trento... 30
Trento Calcio 1921............................ 34
Trento railway station 35
University of Trento.......................... 35

Introduction

Purchase of this book entitles you to a free trial membership in the publisher's book club at www.booksllc.net. (Time limited offer.) Simply enter the barcode number from the back cover onto the membership form. The book club entitles you to select from hundreds of thousands of books at no additional charge. You can also download a digital copy of this and related books to read on the go. Simply enter the title or subject onto the search form to find them.

Each chapter in this book ends with a URL to a hyperlinked online version. Type the URL exactly as it appears. If you change the URL's capitalization it won't work. Use the online version to access related pages, websites, footnotes, tables, color photos, updates. Click the version history tab to see the chapter's contributors. Click the edit link to suggest changes.

A large and diverse editor base collaboratively wrote the book, not a single author. After a long process of discussion and debate, the chapters gradually took on a neutral point of view reached through consensus. Additional editors expanded and contributed to chapters striving to achieve balance and comprehensive coverage. This reduced the regional or cultural bias found in many other books and provided access and breadth on subject matter otherwise little documented.

Adolph Giesl-Gieslingen

Adolph Giesl-Gieslingen (September 7, 1903 - February 11, 1992) was an Austrian locomotive designer and engineer.

Giesl-Gieslingen was born in 1903 in Trient, Tirol, and studied at the Technical College in Vienna. In 1924 he published a technical article on smokebox design and chimneys. In 1925 he received his diploma as an engineer, and began working as a design engineer at the Floridsdorf locomotive works, where he was involved in the construction of the Class 214 2-8-4s. While at Floridorf he continued his studies, being interested in developing the rectangular chimney design developed by Golsdorf in Austria, and finished his doctoral thesis on locomotive front-end design in 1929. In the same year the director, Arno Demmer, sent him to the USA, where he stayed until 1938, working on the New York Central testing a Kylala blastpipe. There he got to know his wife, whom he married in 1933 in New York. After his return is became Demmer's assistant and, after the Second World War, chief engineer of the Floridsdorf company. In 1946 he took up his post as honorary professor at the Technical College in Vienna as the successor to Johann Rihosek.

He developed the Giesl ejector for steam locomotives, which he patented and allowed to be sold by the Schoeller-Bleckmann works. The first notable application of this was to an Austrian 2-8-4 where fitting of the Giesl ejector produced a 25% increase in power output and a small saving in coal. As a result, Giesl ejectors were fitted to locomotives in Austria, East Germany, East Africa and Czechoslovakia. British Railways 9F locomotive No. 92250 was tested at Rugby with a Giesl ejector which demonstrated its effectiveness but due to imminent dieselisation no other locomotives were so fitted. Giesl later published several books on the subject of steam locomotive technology through the Viennese publishers of Verlag Slezak. He died on 11 February 1992 in Vienna.

The effectiveness of the Giesl ejector, being slightly better than the Kylchap exhaust, has led to two preserved locomotives in the UK being fitted with one; Bulleid Pacific No. 34092 *City of Wells* and BR standard class 2 2-6-0 No. 78022.

Source (edited): "http://en.wikipedia.org/wiki/Adolph_Giesl-Gieslingen"

Adriana Volpe

Adriana Volpe (May 31, 1973, Trento, Italy) is a former Italian model, showgirl and actress.

Biography

After scientific high school, she moves to Rome, where in 1990 begins the model profession, managing to model in various capitals of fashion: Milan, Paris, Zurich, Tokyo. In 1992 is taken by RAI to participate as showgirl of the program *Scommettiamo che...*, remaining until 1995, when she debuted on the big screen with the movies *Viaggi di nozze* by Carlo Verdone, where she plays the role of *Marcella*, and Croce e delizia, directed by Luciano De Crescenzo, in the role of *Barbara*.

From 1996 to 1998 goes to Telemontecarlo where she hosts the youth program *The Lion Network*. From 1999 comes back in Rai to take part in the weekend program *Mezzogiorno famiglia*, aired on Rai Due. From 2003 to June 2009 hosts *Mezzogiorno in famiglia* and *Mattina in famiglia*.

Presenter and author of *In forma Rimini Fitness*, broadcasted in 2004 on Rai Due, in the same year she enters the *Albo dei giornalisti* (Journalists Association). In 2005 makes a glamour calendar for the weekly *Panorama*. In 2007 is one of the competitors of the second edition of *Notti sul ghiaccio*

From September 2009 hosts on Rai Due the program of Michele Guardì, *I fatti vostri*.

Private life

The 6 July 2008 the presenter married to businessman Roberto Parli, after an engagement that lasted a little more than a year. She is a great supporter of the S.S. Lazio.

Filmography

Cinema

- *Croce e delizia* (1995), directed by Luciano De Crescenzo - Role: Barbara
- *Viaggi di nozze* (1995), directed by Carlo Verdone - Role: Marcella
- *Arresti domiciliari* (2000), directed by Stefano Calvagna - Role: Bar girl

Source (edited): "http://en.wikipedia.org/wiki/Adriana_Volpe"

Alessandro Bonetti

Alessandro Bonetti (born 10 April 1985 in Trento) is an Italian racing driver. He has competed in such series as International GT Open and the Formula Renault 3.5 Series. He has won races in both the 3000 Pro Series and Le Mans Series.

Source (edited): "http://en.wikipedia.org/wiki/Alessandro_Bonetti"

Alessandro Vittoria

Alessandro Vittoria portrayed by Giovanni Battista Moroni

Alessandro Vittoria (1525–1608) was an Italian Mannerist sculptor of the Venetian school, "one of the main representatives of the Venetian classical style" and rivalling Giambologna as the foremost sculptors of the late 16th century in Italy.

Vittoria was born in the Italian city of Trent and was the son of a tailor. Vittoria was trained in the atelier of the architect-sculptor Jacopo Sansovino; he was a contemporary of Titian whose influence can be detected in his compositions. He was a virtuoso in terracotta, often presented with gilded surfaces, marble and bronze. Like all Italian sculptors of his generation, Vittoria was influenced also by Michelangelo and by the Florentine Mannerist, Bartolomeo Ammanati. The closeness of his associations in projects by architects Sansovino, Sanmicheli and Palladio, working with painters Titian, Tintoretto and Veronese placed him squarely among the protagonists of the Cinquecento art world in late 16th-century Venice.

A Lady of the Zorzi Family, terra cotta of 1570/1580 in the National Gallery of Art.

Vittoria was first trained in his native city, Trento, then moved to Venice, where his long artistic relationship with Sansovino was a stormy one. After one quarrel with Sansovino, he removed from Venice and worked in Vicenza, where he collaborated with Veronese on the decorations of the Villa Barbaro at Maser (1560–62) before returning. The two masters worked jointly on great sculptural commissions until Sansovino's death. Vittoria took up his studio and completed Sansovino's unfinished commissions. One of his pupils was Camillo Mariani.

He died at Venice in 1608. His tomb, with his self-portrait bust, is in the church of San Zaccaria.

Vittoria is known for his classicising portrait busts, a genre that scarcely existed in Venice before him, and for medals as well as for his full-length figures, some of which surmount Sansovino's *Biblioteca Marciana*.

Source (edited): "http://en.wikipedia.org/wiki/Alessandro_Vittoria"

Andrea Pozzo

Andrea Pozzo (Latinized version: *Andreas Puteus*; 30 November 1642, Trento, Italy - 31 August 1709, Vienna, Austria) was an Italian Jesuit Brother, Baroque painter and architect, decorator, stage designer, and art theoretician. He was best known for his grandiose frescoes using illusionistic technique called quadratura, in which architecture and fancy are intermixed. His masterpiece is the nave ceiling of the Church of Sant'Ignazio in Rome. Through his techniques, he has become one of the most remarkable figures of the Baroque period.

Early years

Born in Trento (then under Austrian rule), he did his Humanities at the local Jesuit High School. Showing artistic inclinations he was sent by his father to work with an artist; Pozzo was then 17 years old (in 1659). From aspects of his early style this initial artistic training came probably from Palma il Giovane. After three years he passed under the guidance of another unidentified painter from the workshop of Andrea Sacchi who appears to have taught him the techniques of Roman High Baroque. He would later travel to Como and Milan.

As a Jesuit

Andrea Pozzo's painted ceiling in the Church of St. Ignazio.

On 25 December 1665, he entered the Jesuit Order as a lay brother. In 1668, he was assigned to the *Casa Professa of San Fidele* in Milan, where his festival decorations in honour of Francis Borgia recently canonised (1671) met general approval. He continued artistic training in Genoa and Venice. His early paintings attest the influence of the Lombard School: rich colour, graphic chiaroscuro. When he painted in Genoa the *Life of Jesus* for the *Congregazione de' Mercanti*, he was undoubtedly inspired by Peter Paul Rubens.

Decorating churches

His artistic activity was related to the new (relative to Catholic Church's medieval monastic orders) Order's enormous artistic needs; since many of the Jesuit churches were built in recent decades and were devoid of painted decoration. He was frequently employed by the Jesuits to decorate churches and buildings such as their churches of Modena, Bologna and Arezzo. In 1676, he decorated the interior of San Francis Xavier church in Mondovì. In this church one can already see his later illusionistic techniques: fake gilding, bronze-coloured statues, marbled columns and a trompe-l'oeil dome on a flat ceiling, peopled with foreshortened figures in architectural settings. This was his first large fresco.

In Turin (1678), he painted the ceiling of the Jesuit church of SS. Martiri. The frescoes gradually deteriorated through water infiltration. They were replaced in 1844 by new paintings by Luigi Vacca. Only fragments of the original frescoes survive.

Called to Rome

In 1681, Pozzo was called to Rome by Giovanni Paolo Oliva, Superior General of the Jesuits. Among others, Pozzo worked for Livio Odescalchi, the powerful nephew of the pope, Innocent XI. Initially he was used as a stage designer for biblical pageants, but his illusionistic paintings in perspective for these stages gave him soon a reputation as a virtuoso in wall and ceiling decorations.

The Gesù rooms

His first Roman frescoes were in the corridor linking the Church of the Gesù to the rooms where St.Ignatius had lived. His trompe l'oeil architecture and paintings depicting the Saint's life for the *Camere di San Ignazio* (1681–1686), blended well with already existing paintings by Giacomo Borgognone.

The St Ignatius' Church

His masterpiece, the illusory perspectives in frescoes of the dome, the apse and the ceiling of Rome's Jesuit church of Sant'Ignazio (*illustrations right and below*) were painted between 1685–1694 and are a remarkable and emblematic creation of High Roman Baroque. For several generations, they set the standard for the decoration of Late Baroque ceiling frescos throughout Catholic Europe. Compare this work to Gaulli's masterpiece in the other major Jesuit church in Rome, Il Gesù.

The project had not started upon the church's completion; Sant'Ignazio remained unfinished even after its consecration in 1642. Disputes with the original donors, the Ludovisi, had stopped construction of the planned dome. Pozzo expediently proposed to make an illusionistic dome, when viewed from inside, by painting on canvas. It was impressive to viewers, but controversial; some feared the canvas would soon darken.

On the flat ceiling he painted an allegory of the *Apotheosis of S. Ignatius*, in breathtaking perspective. The painting, 17 m in diameter, is devised to make an observer, looking from a spot marked by a brass disc set into the floor of the nave, seem to see a lofty vaulted roof decorated by statues, while in fact the ceiling is flat. The painting celebrates the missionary spirit of two centuries of adventurous apostolic spirit of Jesuit explorers and missionaries. To modern sensitivity, this would appear to incentivate the expansion of Roman Catholicism, along with the overseas enterprises of the day, to other continents. It was also a combative Catholicism. For example, in the pendentives rather than placing the usual evangelists or scholarly pillars of doctrine, he depicted the victorious warriors of the old testament: *Judith and Holofernes*; *David and Goliath*; Jael and Sisera; and *Samson and the Philistines*. It is said that when completed, some said (sic)*"Sant'Ignazio was a good place to buy meat, since four new butchers are now there."*

In the nave fresco, Light comes from God the Father to the Son who transmits it to St. Ignatius, whence it breaks into four rays leading to the four continents. Pozzo explained that he illustrated the words of Christ in Luke: *I am come to send fire on the earth*, and the words of Ignatius: *Go and set everything aflame*. A further ray illuminates the name of Jesus (2). With its perspective, space-enlarging illusory architecture and with the apparition of the heavenly assembly whirling above, the ensemble offered an example which was copied in several Italian, Austrian, German and Central European churches of the Jesuit order.

The illustionistic perspective of Pozzo's brilliant *trompe-l'oeil* dome at Sant'Ignazio (1685) is revealed by viewing it from the opposite end

The architecture of the trompe-l'oeil dome (*illustration, left*) seems to erase and raise the ceiling with such a realistic impression that it is difficult to distinguish what is real or not. Andrea Pozzo painted this ceiling and trompe-l'oeil dome on a canvas, 17 m wide. The paintings in the apse depict scenes from the life of St. Ignatius, St Francis Xavier and St Francis Borgia.

St Ignatius chapel (Gesù)

In 1695 he was given the prestigious commission, after winning a competition against Sebastiano Cipriani and Giovanni Battista Origone, for an altar in the St. Ignatius chapel in the left transept of the Church of the Gesù. This grandiose altar above the tomb of the saint, built with rare marbles and precious metals, shows the Trinity, while four lapis lazuli columns (these are now copies) enclose the colossal statue of the saint by Pierre Legros. It was the coordinated work of more than 100 sculptors and craftsmen, among them Pierre Legros, Bernardino Ludovisi, Il Lorenzone and Jean-Baptiste Théodon. Andrea Pozzo also designed the altar in the Chapel of St Francesco Borgia in the same church.

Altars in St Ignatius church

In 1697 he was asked to build similar Baroque altars with scenes from the life of St Ignatius in the apse of the Sant'Ignazio church in Rome. These altars house the relics of St. Aloysius Gonzaga and of St. John Berchmans.

Other works of art

Meanwhile he continued painting frescoes and illusory domes in Turin, Mondovì, Modena, Montepulciano and Arezzo. In 1681 he was asked by Cosimo III de' Medici, Grand Duke of Tuscany to paint his self-portrait for the ducal collection (now in the Uffizi in Florence). This oil on canvas has become a most original self-portrait. It shows the painter in a diagonal pose, showing with his right index finger his illusionist easel painting (a trompe-l'oeil dome, perhaps of the Badia church in Arezzo) while his left hand rests on three books (probably alluding to his not-yet published treatises on perspective). The painting was sent to the duke in 1688. He also painted scenes from the life of St Stanislaus Kostka in the saint's rooms of the Jesuit noviciate of Sant'Andrea al Quirinale in Rome.

In Vienna

In 1694 Andrea Pozzo had explained his illusory techniques in a letter to Anton Florian, Prince of Liechtenstein and ambassador of Emperor Leopold I to the Papal Court in Rome. Recommended by Prince Liechtenstein to the emperor, Andrea Pozzo, on the invitation of Leopold I, moved in 1702 (1703?) to Vienna. There he worked for the sovereign, the court, Prince Johann Adam von Liechtenstein, and various religious orders and churches, such as the frescoes and the trompe-l'oeil dome in the Jesuit Church. Some of his tasks were of a decorative, occasional character (church and theatre scenery), and these were soon destroyed.

His most significant surviving work in Vienna is the monumental ceiling fresco of the Hercules Hall of the Liechtenstein garden palace (1707), an *Admittance of Hercules to Olympus*, which, according to the sources, was very admired by contemporaries. Through illusionistic effects, the architectural painting starts unfolding at the border of the ceiling, while the ceiling seems to open up into a heavenly realm filled with olympian gods.

Some of his Viennese altarpieces have also survived (Vienna's Jesuit church). His compositions of altarpieces and illusory ceiling frescoes had a strong influence on the Baroque art in Vienna. He also had many followers in Hungary, Bohemia, Moravia, Slovakia, and even in Poland. His canvases show him to be a far less compelling a painter at close inspection.

Writings

Pozzo published his artistic ideas in a noted theoretical work, entitled *Perspectiva pictorum et architectorum* (2 volumes, 1693, 1698) illustrated with 118 engravings, dedicated to emperor Leopold I. In it he offered instruction in painting architectural perspectives and stage-sets. The work was one of the earliest manuals on perspective for artists and architects and went into many editions, even into the nineteenth century, and has been translated from the original Latin and Italian into numerous languages such as French, German, English and, Chinese thanks to Pozzo's Jesuit connection.

Fresco with *trompe l'œil* dome painted on low vaulting, Jesuit Church, Vienna, Austria

Architect

There are a few architectural designs in

his book *Perspectiva pictorum et architectorum*, indicating that he didn't make any designs before 1690. These designs were not realized, but the design for the S. Apollinare church in Rome was used for the Jesuit church of S Francesco Saverio (1700–1702) in Trento. The interior of this church was equally designed by Pozzo.

At about the same time, between 1701 and 1702, he designed the Jesuit churches of San Bernardo and Chiesa del Gesù in Montepulciano. But his plans for the last church were only partly realized. He is also noted for the construction of the cathedral of St. Nicholas in Ljubljana (1708), inspired by the designs of the Jesuit churches Il Gesù and S. Ignazio in Rome.

Death

He died in Vienna in 1709 at a moment when he intended to return to Italy to design a new Jesuit church in Venice. He was buried with great honours in one of his best realisations, the Jesuit church in Vienna.

His brother, Giuseppe Pozzo, became a barefooted and Carmelite monk of Venice, and was also a painter. He decorated the high altar of the church of the Scalzi in that city during the last years of the 17th century.

Source (edited): "http://en.wikipedia.org/wiki/Andrea_Pozzo"

Andrea Stoppini

Andrea Stoppini (born February 29, 1980 in Trento, Italy) is an Italian professional tennis player.

Stoppini's highest singles ranking has been **World Number 170** on July 6, 2009. In the first round of the 2009 Australian Open, Stoppini lost to defending champion Novak Đoković, 6–3, 6–2, 7–5. Stoppini is a righty who turned professional in 1998. Currently residing in his city of birth, Trento, Stoppini is 3–6 in main tour appearances.

Making his first appearance at Wimbledon in 2009, he beat the top seeded qualifier Sergiy Stakhovsky from Ukraine 2-6, 6-3, 6-3, in the First Qualifying Round, Marcus Willis from Great Britain 6-2, 6-4 in the Second Qualifying Round before losing to Rajeev Ram 6-4, 6-2, 6-4 in the Third Qualifying Round.

Source (edited): "http://en.wikipedia.org/wiki/Andrea_Stoppini"

Antonio da Trento

Antonio da Trento, *Tiburtine Sibyl and the Emperor Augustus*

Antonio da Trento (1508–1550) was an Italian engraver.

Da Trento was born in Trento. He specialized in chiaroscuro wood carving, especially of religious themes and scenes . Da Trento probably first learned wood engraving from Ugo da Carpi. He later was a disciple of Parmigianino, and later within the School of Fontainebleau.

Da Trento's technique involved creating three separate blocks for each print. The first was for the outlines, the second for shadows, and the third was for the lighter tints. Three documented works of his are *The Beheading of St. Peter and St. Paul*, *The Tiburtine Sibyl showing the Virgin Mary, with the Infant Christ*, and *Psyche Saluted by the People with the Honors of Divinity*.

Source (edited): "http://en.wikipedia.org/wiki/Antonio_da_Trento"

Beniamino Andreatta

Beniamino (Nino) Andreatta (August 11, 1928 – March 26, 2007) was an Italian economist and politician.

He was a leftish Christian Democrat and one of the founders of the Italian People's Party in 1994.

Andreatta was born in Trento. He was member of Parliament from 1976 to 1992 and from 1994 to 2001 (Senator from 1976 to 1983, Deputy from 1983-87, again Senator from 1987 to 1992 and finally Deputy from 1994 to 2001). He was member of the European Parliament from 1984 to 1989 and Vice-President of the European People's Party from 1984 to 1987.

He was Minister of Budget from 1979 to 1980, of Treasury from 1980 to 1982, of Foreign Affairs from 1993 to 1994, and of Defense from 1996 to 1998.

His followers included Romano Prodi and Enrico Letta. He is considered to be the architect of the Olive Tree coalition and of the candidacy of Romano Prodi for Prime Minister of Italy in 1996.

He had been in a deep coma since 1999. He died in Bologna.

Source (edited): "http://en.wikipedia.org/wiki/Beniamino_Andreatta"

Bice Bones

Bice Bones (born 1969) is an Italian ski mountaineer.

Selected results

- 1995:
  - 1st, Dolomiti Cup single
  - 1st, Lagorai – Cima d'Asta – Memorial „Egidio Battisti – Lino Vesco
- 1996:
  - 1st, Dolomiti Cup single
  - 1st, Lagorai – Cima d'Asta – Memorial „Egidio Battisti – Lino Vesco
  - 3rd, Sellaronda ski marathon (together with Valentina Cecini)
- 1997:
  - 1st, Trofeo Mezzalama (together with Brunella Parolini and Fabiana Battel)
  - 1st, Dolomiti Cup team race (together with Brunella Parolini)
  - 1st, Lagorai – Cima d'Asta – Memorial „Egidio Battisti – Lino Vesco
  - 2nd, Sellaronda ski marathon (together with Brunella Parolini)
- 1998:
  - 1st, Sellaronda ski marathon (together with Brunella Parolini)
- 1999:
  - 1st, Dolomiti Cup single
  - 1st, Lagorai – Cima d'Asta – Memorial „Egidio Battisti – Lino Vesco
  - 2nd, Sellaronda ski marathon (together with Mirella Fioretta)
- 2001:
  - 1st, Dolomiti Cup team (together with Annamaria Baudena)
  - 1st, Lagorai – Cima d'Asta – Memorial „Egidio Battisti – Lino Vesco
  - 2nd, Sellaronda ski marathon (together with Marika Fusi)
- 2002:
  - 1st, Sellaronda ski marathon (together with Alexander Gretchen)
  - 9th, World Championship team race (together with Annamaria Baudena)
- 2007:
  - 2nd, Ski Alp Val Rendena

Source (edited): "http://en.wikipedia.org/wiki/Bice_Bones"

Cesare Battisti (politician)

Bust of Cesare Battisti by Adolfo Wildt at the Bolzano Victory Monument

Cesare Battisti (4 February 1875 – 12 July 1916) was an Italian politician who became a prominent Irrendentist at the start of the First World War.

Biography

He was born the son of a merchant at Trento, a city with a predominantly Italian-speaking population, which at the time was part of the crown land of Tyrol in Austria-Hungary. Battisti attended the University of Florence where is started to follow the Italian irredentism ideals for his Trentino and, a journalist by profession, won office both municipally and in the County of Tyrol. He was elected to the Tyrolean Landtag at Innsbruck and to the Austrian Reichsrat at Vienna in 1911 as a Socialist representative.

Disgruntled by Austro-Hungarian attitudes to minorities in their empire, Battisti agreed to construct a military guide for the Italians to Austrian provinces that bordered Italy. When Austria-Hungary mobilised in August 1914, Battisti fled to the Kingdom of Italy with his family where he held public meetings demanding Italy attack Austria.

With Italy's belated entry into World War I following the 1915 London Pact, though still an Austro-Hungarian citizen, Battisti fought against the Austro-Hungarian Army in the Alpini Corps at the Italian Front.

Cesare Battisti is remembered in one of the main squares of Rome

After the Battle of Asiago he was captured by the Austrian forces on 10 July 1916 and faced a court-martial in his hometown Trento at the Castello del Buonconsiglio, charged with high treason. Sentenced to death by strangulation, he requested a military execution by firing squad so as to not dishonor the Italian Army uniform. The judge denied his request, and instead procured for him some shabby civilian clothes. Dressed in these, he was executed (hanged and garrotted) the next day, the brutality of which was increased by the fact that the executioner Joseph Lang botched the job and Battisti actually was hanged twice.

The smiling execution squad posed with his body for photographs, which later published did severe damage to the Austrian reputation.

Battisti is considered a national hero in Italy, and a memorial monument was dedicated to him in his hometown.
Source (edited): "http://en.wikipedia.org/wiki/Cesare_Battisti_(politician)"

Cesare Maestri

Cesare Maestri (born 2 October 1929) is an Italian mountaineer and writer.

He was born in Trento in the Italian region of Trentino-Alto Adige/Südtirol. He began climbing in the Dolomites, where he repeated many famous routes, often climbing them solo and free, and put up many new routes of the hardest difficulty, for which he was nicknamed the "Spider of the Dolomites". He became an Alpine Guide in 1952. His notable solos include the Solleder route on the Civetta, the Solda-Conforto Route on the Marmolada, and the southwest ridge of the Matterhorn in winter.

In 1959, Maestri, together with Cesarino Fava and Austrian guide Toni Egger, travelled to Patagonia to attempt the north-east ridge of the unclimbed Cerro Torre. The three climbed up a steep corner below the Col of Conquest (between Cerro Torre and Torre Egger), then Fava turned back and Maestri and Egger headed for the summit. Six days later Fava found Maestri lying face down and almost buried in the snow. They returned to base camp and claimed that Maestri and Egger had reached the summit but Egger had been swept to his death by an avalanche as they were descending.

In 1970, Maestri returned to Cerro Torre and climbed a new route on the south-east side of the mountain, the "Compressor Route", so-called because he used a petrol-driven compressor to power a drill that he used to place a ladder of bolts up blank sections of the rock. On this second endavour, Maestri stopped short of the summit's "ice mushroom", almost always covering the highest point.

Over time, many climbers have started doubting Maestri's 1959 account, as it became evident how difficult, even by today's standards, the alleged route is. Among the doubters are many well-known alpinists like, Carlo Mauri, who had failed to climb the mountain in 1958, Reinhold Messner, and Ermanno Salvaterra, who used to defend Maestri until having attempted the route himself. The criticism was also taken up by British climber and writer Ken Wilson, editor of *Mountain* magazine. Apart from the sheer hardness of the climb, the critics point out that Maestri's description of his route is detailed and accurate up to the high point where Cesarino Fava turned back, but vague and impossible to trace on the mountain thereafter; and that bolts, pitons, fixed ropes and other equipment abandoned by the 1959 expedition is plentiful up to the col, but absent thereafter. Nevertheless, Maestri has consistently maintained his version of events, as did Fava, who died in April 2008.
Source (edited): "http://en.wikipedia.org/wiki/Cesare_Maestri"

Chiara Lubich

Chiara Lubich (22 January 1920 – 14 March 2008) was an Italian Catholic activist and leader and foundress of the Focolare Movement.

Early life

Chiara Lubich was born as **Silvia Lubich** in Trento. Her father lost his job because of the socialist ideas that he held during Italy's period of Fascism. Consequently, the Lubichs lived for years in extreme poverty. To pay for her university studies in philosophy, Lubich tutored other students in Venice and during the 1940s began teaching at an elementary school in Trent.

During World War II, while bombs were destroying Trent, Lubich had a powerful religious experience, 'stronger than the bombs that were falling on Trent' which Lubich immediately communicated to her closest friends. After convincing her friends they declared that, should they be killed, they wished to have only one inscription carved on their tomb: "And we have believed in love".

Her experience led her on 7 December 1943 to change her name to Chiara, in honour of the Saint from Assisi. This date is considered the beginning of the Focolare movement.

These Focolare (small communities of lay volunteers) seek to contribute to peace and to achieve the evangelical unity of all people in every social environment. The goal became a world living in unity, and its spirituality has helped dismantle centuries-old prejudices. Today its members are thousands of people who profess no particular religion.

In her life the day of 13 May 1944 remains the night of one of the most violent bombings of Trent. Lubich's house was among the many buildings destroyed. She decided to stay in Trent to help the new lives being born. She encountered a woman who had lost her senses through the suffering caused by the death of her four children. It was among the poor of Trent that which Lubich often calls the "divine adventure" began.

In 1948 Lubich met the Italian member of Parliament Igino Giordani, writer, journalist, pioneer in the field of ecumenism. He was the co-founder, with Lubich, of the movement, they also gave rise to the New Families Movement and the New Humanity Movement.

1949 marked the first encounter between Lubich and Pasquale Foresi. He was the first Focolarino to become a priest. He helped to progress the Movement's theological studies, and started the Città Nuova Publishing House and also helped to build the small town of Loppiano. Throughout the Movement's development, he has given a contribution to its ecclesiastical and lay expressions. Along with Lubich and Igino Giordani, he is considered a co-founder of the Movement.

In 1954 Lubich met, in Vigo di Fassa (near Trent), with escapees from the forced labour camps in Eastern Europe and after 1960 the Movement began to take shape clandestinely in those countries.

In 1959, at the Mariapolis (summer gathering of the Movement) in the Dolomite Mountains, Lubich addressed a group of politicians inviting them to go beyond the boundaries of their respective nations and to "love the nation of the other as you love your own". Internationalism became a hallmark of the Movement which rapidly spread, firstly in Italy, and afterwards, since 1952, throughout Europe, and since 1959 to other continents. "Little towns" began to be born from 1965 on, with the birth of the first in Loppiano, together with international congresses, and the use of the media contribute to the formation of people who live for the ideal of a "united world". Lubich founded the New Families Movement in 1967.

Chiara Lubich founded the Gen Movement as a youth based movement. (*Gen* standing for New Generation) which animates the wider "Young People for a United World".

In 1966 Chiara Lubich co-founded the school Our Lady, Seat of Wisdom College, Fontem in Cameroon with the assistance of the contemporaneous native chief of Fontem, Fon Fontem Defang. She visited the school in May 2000. The third generation (Gen 3) of the Movement, those who guide the "Youth for Unity" movement, was born in 1970.

1990s

In 1991, shortly after the collapse of the Berlin Wall, during a trip to Brazil, as a response to the situation of those who live in sub-human conditions in the outskirts of the metropolises there, Lubich launched a new project: the "Economy of Communion in Freedom". This quickly developed in various countries involving hundreds of businesses, giving rise to a new economic theory and praxis.

In 1996 Lubich received an Honorary Degree in Social Sciences from the Catholic University of Lublin in Poland. Professor Adam Biela spoke of the "Copernican revolution in the Social Sciences, brought about by her having given life to a 'paradigm of unity' which shows the new psychological, social and economic dimensions which today's post-communist society has been waiting for in this new and difficult transitional phase".

In 1996 Lubich was awarded the UNESCO Prize for education to peace, in Paris, motivated by the fact that, "in an age when ethnic and religious differences too often lead to violent conflict, the spread of the Focolare Movement has also contributed to a constructive dialogue between persons, generations, social classes and peoples."

Lubich was the first Christian, the first lay person, and the first woman to be invited to communicate her spiritual experience to a group of 800 Buddhist monks and nuns in Thailand (January 1997), to 3,000 Black Muslims in the Mosque of Harlem in New York City (May 1997), and to the Jewish community in Buenos Aires (April 1998).

Honorary degrees/Awards

In 1977, Lubich received the Templeton Prize for progress in religion and peace. The presence of many representatives of other religions at the ceremony brought about the beginning of the Movement's inter-religious dialogue.

In 1996, she was also conferred the UNESCO Peace Education Prize.

In May 1997 she visited the United Nations, where she made a speech regarding the unity of peoples in the "Glass Palace". In September 1998 in Strasbourg she was presented with the

1998 Prize for Human Rights by the Council of Europe, for her work "in defence of individual and social rights".

She received honorary degrees in various disciplines: from theology to philosophy, from economics to human and religious sciences, from social science to social communications. These were conferred not only by Catholic universities, but also by lay universities, in Poland, the Philippines, Taiwan, the United States, Mexico, Brazil and Argentina.

Chiara Lubich was honoured with a Doctorate of Divinity (Honoris Causa) from Liverpool Hope University. She thanked the University and provide her hopes for the future: "My most sincere thanks to all at Liverpool Hope University for this doctorate of Divinity in recognition of the Focolare Movement's work in ecumenism and inter-religious dialogue".

Death

She died in Rocca di Papa in her native Italy, aged 88, on 14 March 2008.

Writings

- *Essential Writings: Spirituality Dialogue Culture - New City* (16 Feb 2007) - ISBN 1905039018, ISBN 978-1905039012

Source (edited): "http://en.wikipedia.org/wiki/Chiara_Lubich"

Christoph Anton Migazzi

Count Christoph Cardinal Anton Migazzi (*fully* German: **Christoph Bartholomäus Anton Migazzi, Graf zu Wall und Sonnenthurm**, Italian: *Cristoforo Bartolomeo Antonio Migazzi, conte di Waal e Sonnenthurn*, October 14, 1714, Trento - April 14, 1803, Vienna) was Prince Archbishop of Vienna.

Biography

He was born in 1714, in the county of Tyrol. At nine years of age he entered the school for pages at the residence of Prince Bishop Lamberg at Passau, who later proposed him for admittance to the Collegium Germanicum in Rome. At the age of twenty-two he returned to the Tyrol and devoted himself to the study of civil and canon law.

Cardinal Lamberg took him as conclavist to the conclave of 1740, whence Benedict XIV came forth pope, and to him Cardinal Lamberg earnestly recommended his favourite Migazzi. The latter remained at Rome "in order to quench my thirst for the best science at its very source". By this he meant philosophy as proved by his words spoken about this time: "Without a knowledge of philosophy wit is merely a light fragrance which is soon lost, and erudition a rude formless mass without life or movement, which rolls onward unable to leave any mark of its passage, consuming everything without itself deriving any benefit therefrom." In 1745 he was appointed auditor of the Rota for the German nation.

Owing to the special friendship of Benedict XIV, he was able to conclude several difficult transactions to the entire satisfaction of the Habsburg Empress Maria Theresa, who in return appointed him in 1751 coadjutor to the aged Archbishop of Mechlin. Thereupon consecrated bishop, he was soon removed to Madrid as ambassador in Spain. A treaty which he concluded pleased the empress so much that she appointed him coadjutor of Count Bishop Althan of Waitzen (1756); but as Althan died before his arrival, and six months later Prince Archbishop Trantson also died in Vienna, the empress named Migazzi his successor.

In 1761 Maria Theresa made him administrator for life of the See of Waitzen, and at the same time obtained the cardinal's purple for him from Clement XIII. Migazzi was thus in possession of two sees, the revenues of which he applied to their improvement. In Waitzen he erected the cathedral and episcopal palace and founded the "Collegium pauperum nobilium" and the convent. Indeed he built almost an entire new quarter in that town; it was therefore, to say the least, hard and mortifying when, after twenty-five years of administration the "Concilium locum tenens regium" asked him if there was any priest in his diocese in possession of two benefices or offices, as in that case it was the emperor Joseph II's pleasure that one of them should be given up. Migazzi was forced to resign from Waitzen.

As Archbishop of Vienna time brought him many sorrows. Pious and devoted to the Church as Maria Theresa undoubtedly was, yet during her reign in Austria the so-called Enlightenment era (*Aufklärung*) developed inevitably. Its followers imagined to remedy all the evils of the time and promote in every way the prosperity of mankind. The representatives and the literature of the new movement were everywhere in evidence. Its opponents were denounced as stupid obscurantists and simpletons. "The Masonic lodge of the Three Canons" was printed at Vienna in 1742 and at Prague in 1749 that of the "Three Crowned Stars and Honesty". In a memorial to the empress written in 1769 the archbishop designated as the primary causes of current evils the spirit of the times, atheistic literature, the pernicious influence of many professors, the condition of the censorship, contemporary literature, the contempt of the clergy, the bad example of the nobility, the conduct of affairs of state by irreligious persons and neglect of the observance of holy days. Upon each of these disorders he spoke in noble terms of profound truth. The situation was all the more critical for the Catholic Church since while her means of resistance diminished, her enemies gained adherents.

Meanwhile Pope Clement XIV suppressed the Society of Jesus, but Migazzi endeavoured to save it for Austria. He wrote to the empress, "If the members of the order are dispersed, how can their places be so easily supplied? What expense will be entailed and how many years must pass before the settled condition broken up by the departure of these priests can be restored?" Just twenty years later the cardinal wrote to Francis I, "Even the French envoy who was last here, did not hesitate, as I can prove to your Majesty, to say that if the Jesuits had not been suppressed, France would not have experienced that Revolution so terrible in its consequences." The archbishop opposed as far as they were anticlerical the government monopoly of educational matters, the "enlightened" theology, the "purified" law, the "enlightenment" literature, "tolerance" and encroachment on purely religious matters. He also founded the "Priesterseminar", an establishment for the better preparation of young priests for parochial work. At Rome his influential obtained for the Austrian monarch the privilege of being named in the Canon of the Mass. Migazzi lived to see the election of three popes. Maria Theresa and Kaunitz took a lively interest in his accounts of what transpired in the conclave (23 November 1775-16 February 1776) which elected Pope Pius VI, who subsequently visited Vienna during the reign of Joseph II. He owed his election to Migazzi, leader of the Royalist party. How the empress appreciated Migazzi is sufficiently proved in a letter she wrote to him during the conclave, "I am as ill-humoured as though I had been three months in conclave. I pray for you; but I am often amused to see you imprisoned."

When Frederick II of Prussia heard of the death of the empress he wrote, "Maria Theresa is no more. A new order of things will now begin." Joseph II during his ten years' reign published 6200 laws, court ordinances and decrees affecting the Catholic Church. Even what is judicious in them generally bears the stamp of haste. The first measures, levelled against ecclesiastical jurisdiction, created dissatisfaction as encroachments on the rights of the Church. The number of memorials addressed by Cardinal Migazzi to Joseph II and the government was astonishingly large. He opposed all the Josephist reform decrees injurious to the Church. The "simplified and improved studies", the new methods of ecclesiastical education (general seminaries), interference with the constitutions of religious orders, the suppression of convents and violations of her rights and interference with the matrimonial legislation of the Church, called for vigorous protests on the cardinal's part; but though he protested unceasingly, it was of no avail. Matters did not culminate in a rupture with Rome, Pius VI's visit to Vienna made some impression on the emperor and the Holy See pronounced no solemn condemnation of Josephism. On 12 March, 1790, Leopold, Grand Duke of Tuscany, arrived in Vienna, as successor of his brother Joseph, and as early as 21 March, Migazzi presented him with a memorial concerning the sad condition of the Austrian Church. He mentioned thirteen "grievances" and pointed out for each the means of redress: laxity in monastic discipline, the general seminaries, marriage licenses and the "Religious Commission", which assumed the position of judge of the bishops and their rights. Finding his wishes only partly fulfilled, Migazzi repeatedly expressed his dissatisfaction.

Emperor Francis II, a Christian whose faith and conscience were sincere, ruled his people with fatherly care. In spite of this he confirmed the Josephist system throughout his reign. For nearly a generation the French wars absorbed his attention, during which time the aforesaid "Religious Commission" paid little heed to the representations of the bishops. The cardinal insisted on its abolition. "I am in all things your Majesty's obedient subject, but in spiritual matters the shepherd must say fearlessly that it is a scandal to all Catholics to see such fetters laid upon the bishops. The scandal is even greater when such power is vested in worldly, questionable, even openly dangerous and disreputable men". Age did not diminish his interest even in matters apparently trivial, nor lessen the virile strength of his speech. "The dismal outlook of the Church in your Majesty's dominion is all the more grievous from the fact that one must stand by in idleness, while he realizes how easily the increasing evils could be remedied, how easily your Majesty's conscience could be calmed, the honour of Almighty God, respect for the Faith and the Church of God be secured, the rightful activities of the priesthood set free, and religion and virtue restored to the Catholic people. All this would follow at once, if only your Majesty, setting aside further indecision, would resolve generously and perseveringly to close once for all the sources of so great evils". The emperor in fact made henceforth greater and more numerous concessions, each of which was greeted by Migazzi with satisfaction. When the pilgrimage to Maria Zell, the most famous shrine in Austria, was once more permitted, the cardinal in person led the first procession.

During his long life Migazzi strove with unceasing activity for the welfare of the Church; and he died full of years and of merits on 14 April, 1803 at Vienna. He lies buried in the church of St. Stephen. According to the French writer, Christian Jacq (O Mistério Mozart, Bertand, Portuguese Edition, 2006, a booklet accompanying the historic novel Mozart, O Supremo Mago), Migazzi was one of Mozart's worst enemies and a potential suspect, along with Salieri and rival Masons, of his death by poisoning, in 1791.

Source (edited): "http://en.wikipedia.org/wiki/Christoph_Anton_Migazzi"

Daniel Oss

Daniel Oss (born 13 January 1987 in Trento) is an Italian professional road bicycle racer who is currently racing with Italian Liquigas-Cannondale cycling team on the UCI ProTour.

Biography

In 2004, Oss' first results on the track

and road were outstanding: he excelled in the National Student Track Championships in Pordenone, collecting three podiums in the pursuit; in the same year gained third place in the Madison at the European Student Championships in Fiorenzuola d'Arda.

After a year in the dark, Oss returned to the limelight in 2006 succeeding to finish in five races including Ponton, Isolates Vicentina, Cremona Pessina and Bibano of Godega. In 2007, he won two smaller competitions while in 2008, besides three other competitions, he also participated in the World Championships in Varese, coming home in eighth place in the Under 23 time-trial.

In 2009, Daniel turned professional, joining the team Liquigas; he entered the top 10 for the first time in a professional race during the Tour of Catalunya, it was in the prologue, in which he finished ninth place, four seconds detached from the winner Thor Hushovd. During the same year, he participated in the National Track Championships and came first in the Pursuit along with companions Jacopo Guarnieri, Elijah Viviani and Davide Cimolai. Towards the end of the season, he was able to finish in the top five of a number of professional races: two fourth places in the Tour of Missouri and fifth in the Gran Premio Industria e Commercio di Prato.

In 2010, Oss came fifth in the Gent-Wevelgem and fourth in one of the stages of Three Days of De Panne. He was also involved in his first ever Grand Tour when he came 124th in the Tour de France, he also won the combativity award on Stage 18, for his involvement in the breakaway.

Palmarès

2004
1st Junior National Pursuit Champion
2007
1st Bibano di Godega S. Urbano
2008
2nd, GP Industria del Cuoio e delle Pelli
2010
1st, Giro del Veneto
5th, Gent-Wevelgem
6th Overall, Giro della Provincia di Reggio Calabria
1st, Young rider classification
2011
3rd Overall, Giro della Provincia di Reggio Calabria
1st, Young rider classification

Source (edited): "http://en.wikipedia.org/wiki/Daniel_Oss"

Ernest von Koerber

Ernest von Koerber

Ernest von Koerber (6 November 1850 – 5 March 1919) was an Austrian politician who served as *Ministerpräsident* (prime minister) of the Austrian Empire in 1900 to 1904.

Background

Ernest von Koerber was born in Trento, now part of Italy, then belonging to Austria. His family was ethnically German.

He became extremely involved in Austrian culture and politics. The study of Rechtsstaat, or constitutionality and civil rights was popular during Koerber's teen years and Koerber and his peers such as Sieghart, Steinbach, Baernreither, and Redlich learned and immersed themselves in this principle.

Koerber's knowledge of government was apparent when he launched his career as a bureaucrat in 1874. By 1897 Koerber was a member of the *Reichsrat* (the parliament of Cisleithania, the Austrian portion of Austria-Hungary) and Commerce Minister of Austria. At this time, under the "Dual Monarchy" of Austria-Hungary, there were separate internal governments for Austria and the Kingdom of Hungary. Two years later in 1899 Koerber rose to the position of Minister of the Interior. In 1900, Emperor Franz Joseph asked Koerber to create a cabinet and serve as prime minister. This was by far the most influential position of Koerber's career. Koerber served in this capacity until the end of 1904 when he left office.

First Koerber cabinet

From the beginning of his term in office, Koerber encountered many difficulties. He had full authority only over Cisleithania. Furthermore, the Reichsrat was politically weak. In order to make major liberal reforms Koerber depended largely on Article 14, a provision which allowed the Emperor to issue an "emergency regulation" for any necessary purposes. The meetings of the Reichsrat quickly transformed into forums for Koerber to bargain with party leaders.

Koerber's tenure in office was also marked by tensions within Austria-Hungary. The dual monarchy dissipated any sense of allegiance to a single crown. The various ethnic groups resented one another and it became apparent that most government actions would leave at least one offended group.

In military matters, Koerber opposed providing the Hungarian portion of the army (Honvédség) with its own artillery units. While the emperor advocated such a policy, Koerber sided with Archduke Franz Ferdinand against it, stating that the principle of parity would require the Austrian *Landwehr* to also have artillery, which Austria could not afford.

Even education was a controversial aspect within the monarchy. The Italians in the Habsburg lands could no longer get a university education within the borders of Austria after it lost Veneto in 1866. Koerber sought to fix this problem and presented a draft law establishing an Italian university. However widespread disapproval from Germans culminated in riots during the aborted inauguration of the first course, to be opened in Innsbruck in November 1904 This forced the government to abandon this project.. Koerber also attempted to institute a "National University" with German as the language of teaching but the Italians and Slavs protested this plan.

Koerber pursued reform for the infrastructure of the country, particularly railroads and canals. These expansive reforms were made in efforts to appease the Reichsrat and create a sense of regionalism with non-controversial government reforms. Despite Koerber's efforts, these changes did not provide the reaction Koerber expected and attention once again shifted towards the nationality question..

Additionally, Koerber aimed to promote the industrial and communications sectors. He abolished censorship of the press. Koerber believed this would benefit the changing and expansive monarchy. Koerber also exhibited his liberal ideology by reducing the harsh persecution of Social Democrats, allowing them to organize openly in Austria. This was a tremendous stride in individual rights.

Coupled with these strategies was Koerber's economic savvy. Koerber got the Reichsrat to enact his 1902 economic development program without resorting to article 14. But once again, it was to no avail. Many historians believe that Koerber's emphasis on economic matters over national issues made his administration highly unpopular. Ethnic hostilities ensued despite his attempts at reform. The lack of transition within the state diminished Koerber's dreams and he eventually resigned from office in December 1904. Koerber was succeeded by Paul von Gautsch, Minister of Education.

Second Koerber cabinet

Koerber returned to the spotlight during World War I. From 1915 to 1916, Koerber served as Finance Minister of Austria-Hungary (a "k.u.k" ministry which served both countries). In October 1916, Count Stürgkh, prime minister of Austria, was assassinated. Franz Joseph quickly recalled Koerber to return as prime minister. Many had hoped that Koerber would modify the tyrannical system that had developed during wartime.. However Koerber came into conflict with the new emperor, Charles I and did not make such changes. In fact, the constant disputes made it difficult for Koerber to get anything accomplished. Koerber still held out hope that Austria and Hungary were able to unite, both politically and socially. Charles I, however, continued to take measures that would hinder this progress. Koerber, an aged man by this point, decided he could no longer take these differences. A few short months later Koerber officially retired from office.

He died shortly after the end of the war, on 5 March 1919, in Baden, a town near Vienna.

Source (edited): "http://en.wikipedia.org/wiki/Ernest_von_Koerber"

Francesca Dallapé

Francesca Dallapé (born 24 June 1986 in Trento) is an Italian diver.

Dallapé finished sixth with Noemi Batki in the synchronized 3 metre springboard event of the 2008 Olympic Games.

Source (edited): "http://en.wikipedia.org/wiki/Francesca_Dallap%C3%A9"

Francesca Neri

Francesca Neri (born 10 February 1964) is an Italian actress.

Neri was born in Trento, she has twice received the Silver Ribbon Award for Best Actress from the Italian National Syndicate of Film Journalists, for *Pensavo fosse amore invece era un calesse*, directed by Massimo Troisi (1991) and *Carne trémula (Live Flesh)* (1997).

She has also received three nominations for the David di Donatello Award (Italy's equivalent of the Oscar), as Best Actress in *Il dolce rumore della vita* and *Io amo Andrea* (both 1999) and as Best Supporting Actress for *La felicità non costa niente* (2003).

Other notable films include her three films in Spain: *Live Flesh* (1997, by Pedro Almodóvar, ¡*Dispara!* (*Outrage*, 1993, by Carlos Saura), both with her own voice speaking Spanish, and polemi sex drama film *Las edades de Lulú* (*The Ages of Lulú*, 1990, by Bigas Luna, where she's dubbed into Spanish).

After years of highly acclaimed work in Europe, she first received widespread notice in America when she played the role of Allegra, wife of the Inspector Rinaldo Pazzi in the Hollywood blockbuster, *Hannibal* in 2001. In 2002, she played Colombian wife of Claudio Perrini, and co-starred alongside Arnold Schwarzenegger in *Collateral Damage*.

Neri has one son, Rocco (born 1989), with actor Claudio Amendola.

Source (edited): "http://en.wikipedia.org/wiki/Francesca_Neri"

Francesco Antonio Bonporti

Antonio Bonporti.

Francesco Antonio Bonporti (11 June 1672 – 19 December 1749) was an Italian priest and amateur composer.

He was born in Trento. In 1691, he was admitted in the *Collegium Germanicum* in Rome, where he studied theology. There, he studied composition under the guidance of Giuseppe Ottavio Pitoni and, although it's not confirmed, violin with Arcangelo Corelli.

Back in the native Trento he was ordained a priest in 1695. In 1740 he moved to Padua, where he lived until his death.

He influenced Johann Sebastian Bach in the development of the invention, and in fact several of his works were mistakenly included in a set of Bach's inventions. In reality, Bach had transcribed for harpsichord four violin pieces from Bonporti's op. X (1712).

Bonporti's musical work consists of twelve *opera*, published between 1696 and 1736. He died in Padua in 1749.

Works

This is a listing of his twelve *opera*, first the Italian original generally by Giuseppe Sala in Venice, then the French edition as published by Estienne Roger in Amsterdam and finally the English edition by John Walsh in London. Notice not every *opus* seem to have survived in all languages. As listed in an article published by *Studi Trentini* in 1973, author Clemente Lunelli. His sources on European editions are François Lesure's *Bibliographie des éditions musicales publiées par Estienne Roger...*, Paris, 1969, and William C. Smith's *A bibliography of the musical works published by John Walsh...*, London, 1968.

- Op. 1 - *Suonate a Tre. Due violini, e violoncello obligato...*, 1696. Four parts.
  - *Antoine Bomporti Gentilhomme di Trento opera prima, Sonate à tre, due Violini, Violoncello e basso continuo.* N. 101, 1706, f. 4.0
- Op. 2 -
  - *Antonio Bomporti di Trento, opera seconda, Sonate da Camera à tre, due Violini e Basso continuo.* N. 292, 1701, f. 3.10
  - *Bonporti's Sonata or Chamber Aires in three Parts for two Violins and a Through Bass compos'd by Francisco Antonio Bomporti Opera Seconda (...)* N. 266, c. 1708
  - *Bomporti's Sonata or Chamber Aires (...) Opera Seconda. (...)*, N. 482, c. 1715
- op. 3 - *Motetti a canto solo, con violini (...)*, 1702. Five parts.
- op. 4 -
  - *Antonio Bomporti Opera Quarta, Sonate da Camera à tre, due Violini e basso continuo*, N. 38, 1706, f. 40
  - *Bomporti's Sonata or Chamber Aires (...) Opera Quarto (sic) (...)*, N. 267, c. 1708
- op. 5 *Arie, baletti e correnti* c. 1704 (not extant)
- op. 6 -
  - *Antonio Bomporti, opera sexta, Sonate da Camera à tre, due Violini e basso continuo*, N. 38, 1706, f. 4.0
- op. 7 -
  - *Bomporti opera settima sonate à Violino solo e basso continuo*, N. 303, c. 1707-1708, f. 3.0
  - *10 Solos by Bomporti for a Violin and a Bass*, (Walsh, P. Randall, J. Hare) N. 277d, 1708
  - (?)*Bomportis Solos, for a Violin and a Bass, 4s. od.*, (Walsh) N. 603, c. 1720 or earlier
- op. 8 - (given as lost)
  - *Antonio Bomporti opera ottava, le Triomphe de la grande Aliance à Violon et basse continue*, N. 120, c. 1708-1712, f. 2.0; also mentioned as *Le Triomphe de la grande Aliance, consistent en cent Menuets, composez par Mr. Bomporti opera VIII*
- op. 9 -
  - *Bomporti opera nona, Baletti à Violino solo e basso continuo*, N. 413, f. 1.0; after 1716
- op. 10 - *Invenzioni a violino solo del (...)*, Venice-Trento, Giovanni Parone, 1713. Partiture.
  - *Bomporti opera dècima inventione a Violino solo, e basso contin. (La Pace)*, N. 404, c. 1712-1715, f. 4.0
- op. 11 - *Concerti a quattro, due violini, alto viola, e basso con violino di rinforzo* Trento, Giambattista Monauni, circa 1715. Five parts
- op. 12 - *Concertini e serenate con arie variate, siciliane, recitativi, e chiuse a violino, e violoncello, o cembalo*, Habsburg, Johann Christian Leopold. Partiture.
- *Aria cromatica, e variata a violino violoncello, e cembalo...*, manuscript in the library of the Bruxelles conservatoire, dated 1720. Partiture.
- *Sonata di Buonporti*, manuscript, same as above. Two parts.
- *Six Sonate à deux Flutes et Basse continue, composées par Bomporti et transposées sur la Flute par Corbet*, N. 65, c. 1707-1708, f. 3.0

Source (edited): "http://en.wikipedia.org/wiki/Francesco_Antonio_Bonporti"

Galeazzo von Thun und Hohenstein

Galeazzo von Thun und Hohenstein.

Fra' **Galeazzo von Thun und Hohenstein** (24 September 1850 – 26 March 1931) was the 75th Prince and Grand Master of the Sovereign Military Order of Malta from 1905 to 1931.

Thun und Hohenstein was born in Trento (then in Austria, now in Italy), the youngest son of Count Guidobald Maria Thun und Hohenstein and of his wife, Teresa Guidi dei Marchesi di Bagno.

In 1905 Thun und Hohenstein was elected Grand Master of the Sovereign Military Order of Malta. Under his leadership the order engaged in large-scale hospitaller and charitable activities during World War I. Since he had been born an Austrian subject, Thun und Hohenstein spent much of the war in Austria. He invested a large amount of the order's funds in Austrian war bonds, which became worthless when Austria was defeated. In 1925 he was made a knight of the Spanish branch of the Order of the Golden Fleece.

For the last two years of his life, Thun und Hohenstein was physically incapacitated. He continued to be Grand Master, but a Lieutenant, Pio Franchi de' Cavalieri, acted on his behalf.

Thun und Hohenstein died in Rome.
Source (edited): "http://en.wikipedia.org/wiki/Galeazzo_von_Thun_und_Hohenstein"

Gianna Pederzini

Gianna Pederzini (February 10, 1900, Trento - March 12, 1988, Rome) was an Italian mezzo-soprano.

Pederzini studied in Naples with Fernando de Lucia, and made her stage debut in Messina, as Preziosilla, in 1923. She sang widely in Italy, notably as Mignon and Carmen, and made her debut at the Teatro San Carlo in Naples, as Adalgisa, in 1928, and at the Teatro alla Scala in Milan, in 1930.

Abroad, she appeared at the Royal Opera House in London in 1931, the Opéra de Paris in 1935, the Teatro Colón in 1938, and the Berlin State Opera in 1941.

She defended a wide repertoire, she took part in the 1930s in revivals of rare opereras by Rossini and Donizetti, while singing the standard mezzo roles; Azucena, Ulrica, Amneris, Laura, but also a few dramatic soprano roles such as Santuzza and Fedora, etc.

In the 1950s, she began concentrating on "character roles" such as the Countess in *The Queen of Spades*, Mistress Quickly in *Falstaff*, Madame Flora in *The Medium*, and took part in the creation of *Dialogues of the Carmelites* at La Scala, in 1957.
Source (edited): "http://en.wikipedia.org/wiki/Gianna_Pederzini"

Giorgio Moser

Giorgio Moser (9 October 1923 – 25 September 2004) was an Italian film director and screenwriter. He directed seven films between 1954 and 1996.

Selected filmography
- *Lost Continent* (1954)

Source (edited): "http://en.wikipedia.org/wiki/Giorgio_Moser"

Giovanni Battista Ceschi a Santa Croce

Giovanni Battista Ceschi a Santa Croce

Fra' **Giovanni Battista Ceschi a Santa Croce** (Trento, 1827 – Rome, 24 January 1905) was a leader of the Sovereign Military Order of Malta, succeeding Alessandro Borgia as its lieutenant in 1871, and then being chosen as the 74th Prince and Grand Master in 1879, a decision approved by pope Leo XIII on 28 March that year. This made him the Order's first Grand Master after seventy years of lieutenants and a peripatetic existence - this had begun to end with its becoming permanently based in Rome from 1834 onwards (from about 1889 onwards it also had extraterritorial rights). During his tenure, Ceschi initiated the creation of national lay associations of the order, made up of knights who would remain lay people and not take the Order's vows.

Source (edited): "http://en.wikipedia.org/wiki/Giovanni_Battista_Ceschi_a_Santa_Croce"

Giovanni Kessler

Kessler at the OSCE Parliamentary Assembly

Giovanni Kessler (Trento, June 11, 1956) is an Italian politician of the Democratic Party. President of the Council of the Autonomous Province of Trento from December 2, 2008; since 2010 he seats at the head of the EU Anti-Fraud Office (OLAF).Previously he was a member of the Democratic Left, and before a Christian Democrat. He was a member of the Chamber of Deputies from 2001 to 2006.

Giovanni is the son of Bruno Kessler (1924–1991), former president of the province of Trento and vice-minister to the Interior. He graduated in law at the University of Bologna. In 1985 he became magistrate and was deputy prosecutor in the courts of Trento and Bolzano. Between 1995 and 1996 he worked in Caltanissetta (Sicily) at the anti-mafia Directorate.

He was elected Deputy in 2001, taking part in the Parliamentary Commission of Inquiry on the Telekom Serbia affair (an ungrounded allegation of fraud upon the ruling centre-left government) but was not re-candidated to the next election. He was Vice-President of the Parliamentary Assembly of the Organisation for Security and Cooperation in Europe (OSCE) from 2003 in 2006.

He is a supporter of the Democratic Party and has strongly criticized the choice of Dellai, President of the Autonomous Province of Trento, not to enter the PD in Trentino. In the party primaries, has supported the candidacy of Rosy Bindi against Walter Veltroni.

From September 2006 till August 2008 he was High Commissioner to Combat Counterfeiting, appointed by Romano Prodi as proposed by the Minister of Economic Development Pier Luigi Bersani.

It was elected to the Provincial Council on the 9 November 2008 in the ranks of the Democratic Party of Trentino, obtaining 4789 personal preferences. On December 2, 2008 he was elected chairman of the Council of the Autonomous Province of Trento.

On 20 October 2009 he succeeds to Herwig van Staa (Tyrol) at the head of CALRE (Conference of Regional Legislative Assemblies of 'European Union) with an ambitious programme of improving the ability of regional assemblies to participate in the decision-making of the Union.

In 2009 he starts with Dieter Steger (SVP) and Herwig van Staa (ÖVP), chairmen of the legislative assemblies of South Tyrol and Tyrol, the project of a Euroregion that, for the three territories, would represent a recovery of historical Tyrol. The project takes place October 29, 2009 at the XIV Dreier Landtag. In this joint session, the legislative assemblies of the autonomous provinces of Trentino and South Tyrol and Tyrol unanimously approved the Euroregion Tyrol – South Tyrol – Trentino.

Since December 2010, he seats at the head of OLAF, the Anti-Fraud office of the European Union.

Source (edited): "http://en.wikipedia.org/wiki/Giovanni_Kessler"

Giulia Turco

Giulia Turco, or **Giulia Turco Lazzari** (1848-1912), was a baroness best known as a naturalist and writer in her native Trento, Italy. She was married to the Venetian musician Raffaello Lazzari.

In the 1850s she wrote for the magazine *Rivista delle signorine*, where she published a series of articles and short stories under the pseudonym "Jacopo Turco". Here she began a series of works which can be classified as lifestyle guides for young women and expounded the virtues of travel, charity, floral design, natural medicines and cooking.

Her cultural interests later brought her to support artists and musicians in both, her native Trento and Venice, where she also had a home. Among these were the painter Eugenio Prati, a long time friend, and for whom Turco's diary provides great insight. Another was the naturalist artist Bartolomeo Bezzi, whose "attachment to his native land is a constant aspect of his life and during his stays in Trentino he was a frequent visitor to the cultural circle of Baroness Giulia Turco Lazzari, in such company as Eugenio Prati, Luigi Nono, Angelo dall'Oca Bianca and many other artists, critics, writers and musicians".

By the end of the 19th C. her main focus was on gastronomy and she created a large recipe file and catalogue maintained between 1899 and 1901 with Pellegrino Artusi. In 1904 Artusi published a practical manual for the kitchen, with over 3,000 recipes and 150 tables, simply entitled *Ecco il tuo libro di cucina* (Here is your kitchen book). Turco's participation was anonymous and was only later revealed.

Source (edited): "http://en.wikipedia.org/wiki/Giulia_Turco"

Giulio Alessandrini

Giulio Alessandrini (Latin Julius Alexandrinus or Julius Alexandinus von Neustein; 1506 Trent—25 August 1590 Civezzano) was an Italian physician, author, and poet.

Biography

Giulio Alessandrini studied philosophy and University of Padua. He was physician to emperors Ferdinand I, Maximilian II, and Rudolph II.

He was a devoted follower of Galen and translated many of Galen's works into Latin adding his own commentary.

Works

- *De medicina et medico dialogus.* Zurich, 1557.
- *In Galeni præcipua scripta, annotationes quæ commentariorum loco esse possunt. Accessit Trita illa de theriaca quaestio.* Basel, 1581.
- *Pædotrophia carmine* (1559).
- *Paedotrophia sive de puerorum educatione. Liber ab auctore recognitus. Ejusdem carmina alia.* Trent, 1586.
- *Salubrium, sive de sanitate tuenda, libri triginta tres.* Cologne, 1575 — A treatise on hygiene complied from ancient authors.

Source (edited): "http://en.wikipedia.org/wiki/Giulio_Alessandrini"

Hermann Zingerle

Hermann Zingerle (1870-1935)

Hermann Zingerle (31 March 1870 – 25 April 1935) was an Austrian neurologist and psychiatrist born in Trento.

In 1894 he earned his medical degree from the University of Innsbruck, becoming an assistant at the University of Graz during the following year. In 1899 he received his habilitation for psychiatry and neuropathology, and from 1909 to 1926 was an associate professor at Graz.

His name is associated with Zingerle's automatosis (Zingerle syndrome), a condition in which an individual experiences visual hallucinations taking place during automatic movements and changes in posture. The term "Zingerle syndrome" was named in his honor by Swiss neurologist Georges de Morsier (1894-1982).

Selected publications

- *Ueber die Bedeutung des Balkenmangels im menschlichen Grosshirne* (1898)
- *Erwiderung auf den Aufsatz von Dr. O. von Leonowa-v. Lange: Zur pathologischen Entwickelung des Centralnervensystems* (1904)
- *Untersuchung einer menschlichen Doppelmißbildung (Cephalothoracopag. monosymmetr.) mit besonderer Berücksichtigung des Centralnervensystems* (1907)
- *Über Stellreflexe und Automatische Lageänderungen des Körpers Beim Menschen* (1924)
- *Klinische Studie über Haltungs- und Stellreflexe sowie andere automatische Körperbewegungen beim Menschen. III* (1926)

Source (edited): "http://en.wikipedia.org/wiki/Hermann_Zingerle"

Ida Dalser

Ida Irene Dalser (20 August 1880 – 11 December 1937) was a lover and possibly the first wife of Italian fascist dictator Benito Mussolini.

Early life

Ida Dalser was born in Sopramonte, a village near Trento, the capital of the ethnically Italian Trentino region, at that time within the borders of the Austro-Hungarian Empire. The daughter of the village mayor, she was sent to Paris to study cosmetic medicine, and when she came back she moved to Milan, where she opened a French-style beauty salon.

Marriage and motherhood

It is unclear whether Ida Dalser first met young Benito Mussolini in Trento (where he had found his first job as a journalist in 1909) or in Milan (where he had moved soon afterwards). The two started a relationship and when Mussolini was refused work on the basis of his fervent socialist political activity, she financed him with the revenues of her beautician job. According to some sources, they got married in 1914, and in 1915 she bore him his first child, Benito Albino Mussolini. However, there are no records of this presumptive marriage.

Estrangement and start of legal dispute

The reasons why Mussolini and Dalser grew estranged at some time between their presumptive marriage and the birth of their son remain unclear, although his affair with another woman, Rachele Guidi, may have played a role. When World War I broke out, Mussolini decided to enlist. On December 17, 1915, while an inpatient at a hospital in Treviglio, Mussolini married Rachele Guidi. When this became known to Ida Dalser, a legal dispute began between her and the new couple.

Immediately after his second marriage, Mussolini left Italy to fight in the First World War. While he was on service, the Kingdom of Italy regularly paid Dalser a war pension, and when Mussolini was injured by a mortar shot in 1917, she received a visit from the Carabinieri notifying her that her husband was wounded in action.

Persecution and death

In 1917, Mussolini came back from the war. His political career accelerated: in 1919 he went on to found the Fasci italiani di combattimento, which became the National Fascist Party in 1921; in the latter year he was also elected to the Chamber of Deputies. With the 1922 March on Rome, Mussolini seized power and became a dictator officially recognised by the then ruling House of Savoy.

Once Mussolini was in power, Ida Dalser and her son were placed under surveillance by the police, and paper evidence of their relationship was tracked down to be destroyed by government agents. She still persisted in vocally claiming her role as the dictator's wife, and even publicly denounced Mussolini as a traitor, stating that during his years in Milan he had accepted a bribe from the French government in exchange for political campaigning in support of the involvement of then neutral Italy in the war on the side of France. Eventually, she was forcibly interned in the psychiatric hospital of Pergine Valsugana, and then transferred to that of the island of *San Clemente* in Venice, where she died in 1937. The cause of death was registered as "brain haemorrhage".

Benito Albino's fate

Benito Albino Mussolini was abducted by government agents, told his mother was dead, and was adopted as an orphan by the fascist ex-police chief of Sopramonte. Initially educated at a Barnabite college in Moncalieri, he enrolled in the Italian Royal Navy, and always remained under close surveillance by the fascist government. Still he persisted in stating Benito Mussolini was his father, and was eventually forcibly interned in an asylum in Mombello, Province of Milan, where he died in 1942, aged twenty-six.

Rediscovery and Dalser's life in film

The story of Benito Mussolini's first marriage was suppressed during fascist rule, and remained generally unknown for years afterwards. It was uncovered in 2005 by Italian journalist Marco Zeni and made public through a TV documentary on state television as well as two books (*L'ultimo filò* and *La moglie di Mussolini*).

Vincere, a biopic on Dalser's life, under the direction of Marco Bellocchio, was screened at the 2009 American Film Institute Festival and in competition at the 2009 Cannes Film Festival.
Source (edited): "http://en.wikipedia.org/wiki/Ida_Dalser"

Jacob Acontius

Jacob Acontius (Italian: ***Jacopo*** (or **Giacomo**) **Aconcio**; 7 September 1492 – around 1566) was an Italian jurist, theologian, philosopher and engineer. He is now known for his contribution to the history of religious toleration.

Life

He was traditionally thought to have been born at Trento, although it was probably Ossana.

He was one of the Italians, like Peter Martyr and Bernardino Ochino, who repudiated papal doctrine and ultimately found refuge in England. Like them, his revolt against Romanism took a more extreme form than Lutheranism, and after a temporary residence in Switzerland and at Strasbourg (between 1557 and 1558), he arrived in England soon after Elizabeth's accession (1559). He had studied law and theology, but his profession was that of an engineer, and in this capacity he found employment with the English government.

On his arrival in London he joined the Dutch Reformed Church in Austin Friars, but he was "infected with Anabaptistical and Arian opinions" and was excluded from the sacrament by Edmund Grindal, bishop of London. He was granted naturalization on 8 October 1561. He was for some time occupied with draining Plumstead marshes, for which object various acts of Parliament were passed at this time. In 1564 he was sent to report on the fortifications of Berwick.

Works

Before reaching England he had published a treatise on the methods of investigation, *De Methodo, hoc est, de recte investigandarum tradendarumque Scientiarum ratione* (Basel, 1558, 8vo); and his critical spirit placed him outside all the recognized religious societies of his time. His heterodoxy is revealed in his *Stratagematum Satanae libri octo*, sometimes abbreviated as *Stratagemata Satanae*, published in 1565 and translated into various languages. The *Stratagems of Satan* are the dogmatic creeds which rent the Christian church. Aconcio sought to find the common denominator of the various creeds; this was essential doctrine, the rest was immaterial. To arrive at this common basis, he had to reduce dogma to a low level, and his result was generally repudiated.

Selden applied to Aconcio the remark *ubi bene, nil melius; ubi male, nemo pejus*. The dedication of such a work to Queen Elizabeth illustrates the tolerance or religious laxity during the early years of her reign. Aconcio later found another patron in Robert Dudley, 1st Earl of Leicester, and died about 1566.
Source (edited): "http://en.wikipedia.org/wiki/Jacob_Acontius"

Johann Baptist von Lampi the Younger

Ivan Akimov by Lampi the Younger.

Johann Baptist von Lampi the Younger (1775–1837) was an Austrian portrait painter. He was born at Trento and studied under his father, Johann Baptist von Lampi the Elder, and later at the Academy at Vienna. He went with his father for thirteen years to St. Petersburg, and became a member of the Academy at that city as well as of that at Vienna in 1813. He painted many of the most distinguished personages of his time. He died at Vienna.
Source (edited): "http://en.wikipedia.org/wiki/Johann_Baptist_von_Lampi_the_Younger"

Leonardo Bertagnolli

Leonardo Bertagnolli (born January 8, 1978 in Trento) is an Italian professional road bicycle racer, currently riding for UCI ProTeam Lampre-ISD. He signed for Amica Chips-Knauf, a new team in the 2009 season, though he rode for Diquigiovanni-Androni in the 2009 Giro d'Italia. It is unclear if Bertagnolli switched teams before Amica Chips-Knauf's mid-season collapse or after, and whether he continued with Diquigiovanni-Androni after the Giro or briefly returned to Amica Chips-Knauf.

Palmares
2004
1st, Coppa Placci
1st, Coppa Agostoni
1st, Trofeo dell'Etna
2005
1st, Stage 2, Vuelta a España
1st, Stage 3, Tour du Limousin
2006
1st, Stage 6, Tirreno–Adriatico
1st, Tour du Haut-Var
2007
1st, Clasica de San Sebastián
1st, Memorial Cimurri
4th, 2007 Deutschland Tour
2008
1st, Intaka Tech Worlds View Challenge #2
2009
1st, Stage 15, Giro d'Italia
1st, Stage 2, Brixia Tour
2010
1st, Stage 3, Tour of Austria
2nd Overall Trofeo Matteotti
3rd Coppa Sabatini
Source (edited): "http://en.wikipedia.org/wiki/Leonardo_Bertagnolli"

Leopold Ernst von Firmian

Leopold Ernst von Firmian (1708-1783) was an Austrian bishop and Cardinal.

Leopold Ernst von Firmian (1708-1783)

He was bishop of Seckau from 1739 to 1763, campaigning against Protestantism. He also acted as coadjutor bishop or administrator of the bishopric of Trento, from 1748 to 1758. As Prince-Bishop of Passau from 1763 to 1783, he was a more tolerant reforming Catholic. He became Cardinal of S. Pietro in Montorio in 1772.

Family

His parents were Baron Franz Alfons Georg von Firmian and Countess Barbara Elisabeth von Thun. Leopold Anton Freiherr von Firmian, archbishop of Salzburg, was his uncle.

Source (edited): "http://en.wikipedia.org/wiki/Leopold_Ernst_von_Firmian"

Lorenzo Bernardi

Lorenzo Bernardi (born 11 August 1968) is an Italian volleyball player who was twice World champion with his national team in 1990 and 1994, and was elected "Volleyball Player of the Century" in 2001.

Career

Born in Trento, Bernardi started his long career in the 1980s, and was soon revealed as a multi-talented hitter and excellent passer. From 1985 he played with the Panini Modena club, who was then almost unbeatable in Italy. Bernardi won the Italian championship nine times with Modena and with Sisley Treviso, which he played for from 1990 to 2001.

His first cap with Italian national volleyball team was on 27 May 1987: he played for a total of 306 times in "Azzurri" colours, winning two European gold medals (in 1989 and 1995), two World Championships (1990 and 1994), three Volleyball World Leagues and the Volleyball World Cup in 1995. His international tally also includes two more gold medals, five silver medals and one bronze.

He was elected best player of the 1994 World Championship and 1995 European Championship, and in 2001, the FIVB declared him to be the "Volleyball Player of the Century".

In 2004, he played some competitions in Qatar and after a spell in Greece and Olympiakos SC, he has returned to play in Italy as of November 2005. In spite of his late age of 37, he was declared MVP of the first match in his new Italian club career. In his later career he played for a B1 series (Italy's third category) near his native Trento.

During the 2010/2011 season, he took over the head coach position of the Polish club Jastrzębski Węgiel, and was able to reach the 4th spot in the CEV Champions League

Individual awards

- *1992 FIVB World League "Most Valuable Player"*

Source (edited): "http://en.wikipedia.org/wiki/Lorenzo_Bernardi"

Lorenzo Dellai

Lorenzo Dellai.

Lorenzo Dellai (born November 28, 1959 in Trento) is an Italian politician, the governor of the province of Trento and the President of Trentino-Alto Adige/Südtirol.

In 1990 he was elected for the first time as mayor of Trento, and re-elected in 1995.

In 1998 Lorenzo Dellai founded the Daisy Civic List, a regionalist political party active in the Province of Trento.

Since 1999 Dellai has been the President of the Province of Trento, and since 2006, also the President of Trentino-Alto Adige/Südtirol.

Source (edited): "http://en.wikipedia.org/wiki/Lorenzo_Dellai"

Ludovico Madruzzo

Portrait of Ludovico Madruzzo by Giovanni Battista Moroni. Art Institute, Chicago.

Ludovico Madruzzo (1532–1600) was an Italian Roman Catholic cardinal and statesman, the Imperial crown-cardinal and Prince-Bishop of the Bishopric of Trento (involving the secular rule as well as church duties).

Biography

Born in Trento, he was the son of baron Niccolò Madruzzo and Helene of Lanberg, and nephew of Cristoforo Madruzzo, Prince-Bishop of Trento. He studied at the universities of Leuven and Paris.

In 1550 his uncle Cristoforo, named Governor of Milan, entrusted him the administration of the Bishopric of Trento, where the Council of Trent had been in intermittent progress since 1545; it was to continue until 1563. After numerous important diplomatic and political experiences (including the mourning discourse at Charles V's funeral, he was created cardinal in 1561 by Pope Pius IV, given the titular church of San Callisto. Six years later he was appointed titular of the diocese of Trento.

Under agreements between Bernardo Clesio and Cristoforo Madruzzo, the bishopric had gained a substantial independence from the Habsburg-controlled county of Tyrol, and this caused strife between Ludovico and the Austrian archduke (and future emperor) Ferdinand II. The latter invaded Trentine territory in 1567, and Ludovico moved to Rome, waiting for a diplomatic resolution of the conflict. Trento's authority was totally re-established by the Diet of Speyer in 1587.

Ludovico Madruzzo was a friend of St. Charles Borromeo and St. Philip Neri.

He died in Rome in 1600. He was succeeded by his nephew Carlo Gaudenzio.

Source (edited): "http://en.wikipedia.org/wiki/Ludovico_Madruzzo"

Marcello Guarducci

Marcello Guarducci (born July 11, 1956) is an Italian former freestyle swimmer.

Guarducci won several gold medals in different editions of the Mediterranean Games.

Guarducci participated in three Olympics Games editions reaching finals. Being part of a military athletic group, he missed the games of Moscow 1980 because of the boycott.
Source (edited): "http://en.wikipedia.org/wiki/Marcello_Guarducci"

Margherita Cagol

Margherita Cagol (1945–5 June 1975) was a former leader of the Italian left-wing militant organization, the Red Brigades (*Brigate Rosse*). She was married to Renato Curcio.

Life

She was born to a middle-class family in Sardagna, Trentino, in the north of Italy. Her mother was a pharmacist and her father a prosperous merchant. In 1964 she enrolled in the facolty of Social Science at Trent University. She soon became involved with student movements, where she got to know Renato Curcio. Together with him she worked for the publication *Lavoro Politico* (Political Work). She graduated in 1969. She married in a Catholic ceremony Renato Curcio, after which the couple moved to Milan, where she intended to study for a further two years.

In Milan, the Curcios became full-fledged militants. The Red Brigades were formed with Alberto Franceschini in the second half of 1970 as a result of the merger of Renato Curcio's Proletarian Left and a radical student and worker group. After getting arrested in February 1971 for occupying a vacant house, the Curcios and the most militant members of the Proletarian Left went completely underground and organized the Red Brigades and spent the next three years, from 1972 to 1975, engaging in a series of bombings and kidnappings of prominent figures. Renato Curcio was captured, but freed by Margherita in a raid on the prison five months later, on the 18 February 1975.

In April Cagol, Mario Moretti and Renato Curcio met in a house near Piacenza to discuss their strategy. The movement was growing and they needed further finance to continue the struggle. They decided to follow the example of the South American guerrillas and carry out a series of kidnappings, one of the victims being the industrialist Vallarino Gancia. He was chosen because he was very rich and lived in a region with which they were familiar. According to Renato Curcio, he had also financed a Fascist organization. He was kidnapped on 4 June while on his way to his villa in Canelli, near Asti, bundled into a transporter, and taken to the farmhouse (Cascina Spiotta) on the hills of Acqui Terme. This farmhouse had been purchased some time before by Cagol, and had been used by members of the Red Brigades from Turin. Renato Curcio did not take part in the operation; as a prison escapee, his picture had been published all over Italy, and it was considered too dangerous. Cagol, along with a companion, were left to guard Gancia. Later that evening Cagol phoned Renator to tell him that the operation had been a success. The following morning Carabinieri starting investigating farmhouses in the neighbourhood. Cagol had been on watch during the night, and had gone to bed. Her companion, who took over the watch, fell asleep, and did not wake up until the Carabinieri started knocking at the door. Their escape route was blocked by the Carabinieris' car, so they decided to fight it out. In the ensuing gunfight, two police officers were killed, as was Cagol. Renato Curcio was again captured by the authorities in January 1976, tried, convicted and imprisoned.
Source (edited): "http://en.wikipedia.org/wiki/Margherita_Cagol"

Mariano Piccoli

Mariano Piccoli (born September 11, 1970 in Trento) is an Italian former road bicycle racer.
Source (edited): "http://en.wikipedia.org/wiki/Mariano_Piccoli"

Martino Martini

Martino Martini (simplified Chinese: 卫匡国; traditional Chinese: 衛匡國; pinyin: *Wèi Kuāngguó*) (20 September 1614 – 6 June 1661) was an Italian Jesuit missionary, cartographer and historian, mainly working on imperial China.

Early years

Frontpage of *Novus Atlas sinensis*, by Martino Martini, Amsterdam, 1655.

Martini was born in Trento, in the Bishopric of Trent. After finishing high school studies in Trent in 1631, he entered the Austrian province of the Society of Jesus, from where he was sent to study classical letters and philosophy at the Roman College, Rome (1634–37). However his interest was more in astronomy and mathematics which he studied under Athanasius Kircher. His request to be sent as a missionary to China had already been granted by Mutius Vitelleschi, the then Superior General of the Jesuits. He did his theological studies in Portugal (1637–39)—already on his way to China—where he was ordained priest (1639, in Lisbon).

In the Chinese Empire

He set out for China in 1640, and arrived in Macau in 1642 where he studied Chinese for some time. In 1643 he crossed the border and settled in Hangzhou, Zhejiang Province, from where he did much traveling in view of gathering scientific information, especially on the geography of the Chinese empire: he visited several provinces, as well as Peking and the Great Wall. He made great use of his talents as missionary, scholar, writer and superior.

Soon after Martini's arrival to China, the Ming capital Beijing fell to Li Zicheng's rebels (April, 1644) and then to the Manchus, and the last "real" Ming emperor, the Chongzhen Emperor, hanged himself. Down in Zhenjiang, Martini continued working with the short-lived regime of Zhu Yujian, Prince of Tang, who set himself up as the (Southern) Ming Longwu Emperor. Soon enough, the Manchu troops reached Zhejiang. According to Martini's own report (which appeared in some editions of his *De bello tartarico*), the Jesuit was able to switch his allegiance to China's new masters in an easy enough, but bold, way. When Wenzhou, in southern Zhejiang, where Martini happened to be on a mission for Zhu Yujian, was besieged by the Manchus and was about to fall, the Jesuit decorated the house where he was staying with a large red poster with seven characters saying, "Here lives a doctor of the divine Law who has come from the Great West". Under the poster he set up tables with European books, astronomical instruments, etc., surrounding an altar with an image of Jesus. When the Manchu troops arrived, their commander was sufficiently impressed with the display to approach Martni politely and ask if he'd like to switch his loyalty to the new Qing Dynasty. Martini agreed, and had his head shaved in the Manchu way, and his Chinese dress and hat replaced with Manchu-styles ones. The Manchus then allowed him to return to his Hangzhou church, and provided him and the Hangzhou Christian community with necessary protection.

The Chinese Rites affair

In 1651 Martini left China for Rome as the Delegate of the Chinese Mission Superior. He took advantage of the long, adventurous voyage (going first to the Philippines, from thence on a Dutch privateer to Bergen, Norway, which he reached on the 31 August 1653, and then to Amsterdam). Further, and still on his way to Rome, he met printers in Antwerp, Vienna and Munich to submit to them historical and cartographic data he had prepared. The works were printed and made him famous.

When passing through Leyden, Martini was met by Jacobus Golius, a scholar of Arabic and Persian at the university there. Golius did not know Chinese, but had read about "Cathay" in Persian books, and wanted to verify the truth of the earlier reports of Jesuits such as Matteo Ricci and Bento de Góis who believed that Cathay is the same place as China where they lived or visited. Golius was familiar with the discussion of the "Cathayan" calendar in *Zij-i Ilkhani*, a work by the Persian astronomer Nasir al-Din al-Tusi, completed in 1272. When Golius met Martini (who, of course knew no Persian), the two scholars found that the names of the 12 divisions into which, according to Nasir al-Din, the "Cathayans" were dividing the day, as well as those of the 24 sections of the year reported by Nasir al-Din matched those that Martinini had learned in China. The story, soon published by Martini in the "Additamentum" to his Atlas of China, seemed to have finally convinced most Europeans scholars that China and Cathay were the same.

It is only in the spring of 1655 that Martini reached Rome.

There, in Rome, was the most difficult part of his journey. He had brought along (for the Holy Office of the Church) a long and detailed communication from the Jesuit missionaries in China, in defence of their inculturated missionary and religious approach: the so-called *Chinese Rites* (Veneration of ancestors, and other practices allowed to new Christians). Discussions and debates took place for 5 months, at the end of which the Propaganda Fide issued a decree in favour of the Jesuits (23 March 1656). A battle was won, but the controversy did not abate.

Return to China

In 1658, after a most difficult journey, he was back in China with the favourable decree. He was again involved in pastoral and missionary activities in the Hangzhou area where he built a three naves church that was considered to be one of the most beautiful of the country (1659–61). The church was hardly built when he died of cholera (1661).

Post-mortem phenomena

Martini's grave in Hangzhou

According to the attestation of Prosper Intorcetta (in *Litt. Annuae*, 1861) his body was found undecayed twenty years after; it became a long-standing object of cult not only for Christians, until in 1877, suspecting idolatry, the hierarchy had it buried again.

Contemporary appreciations

Today's scientists are more and more interested in the works of Martini; he is acclaimed as the father of Chinese geographical science. During an international convention organized in the city of Trento (his birthplace) a member of the Chinese academy of Social Sciences, the Professor Ma Yong said : "Martini was the first to study the history and geography of China with rigorous scientific objectivity; the extend of his knowledge of the Chinese culture, the accuracy of his investigations, the depth of his understanding of things Chinese are examples for the modern sinologists". Ferdinand von Richthofen calls Martini "the leading geographer of the Chinese mission, one who was unexcelled and hardly equalled, during the XVIII century…There was no other missionary, either before or after, who made such diligent use of his time in acquiring information about the country". (China, I, 674 sq.)

Works

A European artist's impression of a Manchu warrior devastating China, from the title page of Martini's *Regni Sinensis a Tartaris devastati enarratio*. Modern historians (e.g. Pamela Kyle Crossley in *The Manchu*, or D.E. Mungello) note the discrepancy between the picture and the content of the book; e.g., the severed head held by the warrior has a queue, which is a Manchu hairstyle (also imposed by Manchu on the population of conquered China), and is not likely to be had by a Ming loyalist

- Martini's most important work is *Novus Atlas Sinensis*, which appeared as part of volume 10 of Joan Blaeu's Atlas Maior (Amsterdam 1655). This work, a folio with 17 maps and 171 pages of text was, in the words of the early 20th-century German geographer Ferdinand von Richthofen, *the most complete geographical description of China that we possess, and through which Martini has become the father of geographical learning on China*. The French Jesuits of the time concurred, saying that even du Halde's monumental *Description…de la Chine* did not fully supersede Martini's work. (Scan of the maps of the atlas (not very high resolution), at the National Library of Australia).
- Of the great chronological work which Martini had planned, and which was to comprise the whole Chinese history from the earliest age, only the first part appeared: *Sinicæ Historiæ Decas Prima* (Munich 1658), which reached until the birth of Jesus.
- His *De Bello Tartarico Historia* (Antwerp 1654) is also important as Chinese history, for Martini himself had lived through the frightful occurrences which brought about the overthrow of the ancient Ming dynasty. The works have been repeatedly published and translated into different languages. There is also a later version, entitled *Regni Sinensis a Tartaris devastati enarratio* (1661); compared to the original *De Bello Tartarica Historia*, it has some additions, such as an index.
- Interesting as missionary history is his *Brevis Relatio de Numero et Qualitate Christianorum apud Sinas*, (Brussels, 1654).
- Besides these, Martini wrote a series of theological and apologetical works in Chinese, including a *De Amicitia* (Hangzhou, 1661) that could have been the first anthology of Western authors available in China (Martini's selection fished mainly into Roman and Greek writings).
- Several works, among them a Chinese translation of the works of Francisco Suarez, still exist in his handwriting. Of these is notable his *Grammatica Sinica*, which he brought along and donated to Jacobus Golius, and that couldn't be printed because of the impossibility to reproduce Chinese characters. This very copy is still preserved in the Antwerp Royal Library; over time many others were made.

For his minor writings (published letters to Athanasius Kircher, etc.) see Martino Martini bibliography.

Source (edited): "http://en.wikipedia.org/wiki/Martino_Martini"

Matthias Gallas

Matthias Gallas.

Matthias Gallas, Graf von Campo und Herzog von Lucera (Count of Campo, Duke of Lucera) (b. **Matteo Gallasso** Trento 1584 - Vienna 1647), was an Austrian soldier, who first saw service in Flanders, then in Savoy with the Spaniards, and subsequently joined the forces of the Catholic League as captain during the Thirty Years' War.

On the general outbreak of hostilities in Germany, Gallas, as colonel of an infantry regiment, distinguished himself, especially at the battle of Stadtlohn (1623). In 1630 he was serving as General-Feldwachtmeister under Count Collalto in Italy, and was mainly instrumental in the capture of Mantua in the War of Mantuan Succession. Made count of the Empire for this service, he returned to Germany for the campaign against Gustavus Adolphus. In command of a corps of Wallenstein's army, he covered Bohemia against the Swedes in 1631-1632, and served at the Alte Veste near Nuremberg, and at Lützen. Further good service against Bernhard of Saxe-Weimar commended General Gallas to the notice of the emperor, who made him lieutenant-general in his own army.

Upon being approached by Joachim Friedrich von Blumenthal at the Emperor Ferdinand's behest, he became one of the chief conspirators against Wallenstein, and after the tragedy of Eger was appointed to the command of the army which Wallenstein had formed and led. At the great battle of Nördlingen (August 23, 1634) in which the army of Sweden was almost annihilated, Gallas commanded the victorious Imperialists. His next command was in Lorraine, but even the Moselle valley had suffered so much from the ravages of war that his army perished of want. Still more was this the case in northern Germany, where Gallas commanded against the Swedish general Banér in 1637 and 1638. At first driving the Swedes before him, in the end he made a complete failure of the campaign, lost his command, and was subject to much ridicule.

It was, however, rather the indiscipline of his men (the baneful legacy of Wallenstein's methods) than his own faults which brought about his disastrous retreat across North Germany, and at a moment of crisis he was recalled to endeavour to stop Torstenson's victorious advance, only to be shut up in Magdeburg, whence he escaped with the barest remnant of his forces. Once more relieved of his command, he was again recalled to make head against the Swedes in 1645 (after their victory at Jankow). Before long, old and warworn, he resigned his command, and died in 1647 at Vienna. His army had earned for itself the reputation of being the most cruel and rapacious force even in the Thirty Years' War, and his *Merode Bruder* have survived in the word *marauder*.

Like many other generals of that period, he had acquired much wealth and great territorial possessions (the latter mostly his share of Wallenstein's estates). He was the founder of the Austrian family of Clam-Gallas, which furnished many distinguished soldiers to the Imperial army.

Source (edited): "http://en.wikipedia.org/wiki/Matthias_Gallas"

Mauro Trentini

Mauro Trentini (born 12 September 1975 in Trento) is an Italian former track cyclist, specialising in the pursuit, where he was team pursuit world champion in 1996 and individual pursuit bronze medalist in 1999.

Source (edited): "http://en.wikipedia.org/wiki/Mauro_Trentini"

Mirko Bortolotti

Mirko Bortolotti (born 10 January 1990 in Trento) is an Italian racing driver.

Career

Italian series

After karting for several years, Bortolotti began his formula racing career in 2005 by competing in the Italian Formula Renault Winter Series and Formula Gloria. He competed in the Winter Series for a further two years, with a best finish of fourth in 2006. He also drove in the Italian Formula Junior 1600 championship for this year, in addition to the Formula Azzurra championship. In the latter series he finished as runner-up in the drivers' championship, behind winner Giuseppe Termine.

In 2007, Bortolotti moved up to Italian Formula Three, finishing fourth in the championship at his first attempt. He remained in the series for 2008, driving for the Lucidi Motors team, and won the championship with nine wins and six pole positions from the sixteen races.

Formula Two

Bortolotti obtained backing from Red Bull following his championship win; the company opted to place him in the relaunched FIA Formula Two Championship in 2009. He drove car number 14 in the series, and finished fourth. During the break between the final two rounds of the season, Bortolotti returned to Formula Three to compete for Carlin Motorsport in the Formula Three Euroseries season finale at Hockenheim, finishing on the podium in the second race.

Formula One

As a reward for their performances in the 2008 Italian F3 championship, Bortolotti, Edoardo Piscopo and Salvatore Cicatelli were all given a test of the Ferrari team's F2008 chassis at the Fiorano Circuit in November 2008. Bortolotti impressed by setting a time of 59.111 seconds, quicker than the previous fastest lap set by the F2008 at the circuit by any driver.

In 2009, among several other drivers, Bortolotti was linked to a drive with Ferrari as a replacement for injured Felipe Massa, after poor performances by Luca Badoer.
- * Season in progress.
† - As Bortolotti was a guest driver, he was ineligible to score points.

Complete Formula Two results

(key) (Races in **bold** indicate pole position) (Races in *italics* indicate fastest lap)

Complete Formula Three Euroseries results

(key) (Races in **bold** indicate pole position) (Races in *italics* indicate fastest lap)

Complete Formula Three Euroseries results

Complete GP3 Series results

(key) (Races in **bold** indicate pole position) (Races in *italics* indicate fastest lap)

† Bortolotti did not finish the race, but was classified as he completed over 90% of the race distance.
Source (edited): "http://en.wikipedia.org/wiki/Mirko_Bortolotti"

Paolo Oss Mazzurana

Paolo Oss Mazzurana, in a painting by Ettore Ximenes (1856)

Paolo Oss Mazzurana (1833 - 1895) was an Italian statesman, and most importantly the most famous mayor of his native city, Trento. His tenure was characterized by progressive economic policies that impacted Trento's commercial sector and eventually led to its independence as a state.

History

Mazzurana is considered as the symbol of an age of great progress from the civil and social point of view and from a more strictly economic one of the city and of the entire Trentino. Under his far-sighted guidance Trento was given a modern urbanistic order, became industrialized and realized meaningful cultural and social increase. Thanks to his charisma he realized a series of economic reforms in favour of the population, adopting a political "liberal" address and establishing a creative relationship with Trento, an Italian city in the Habsburg empire. Insofar as the action of Paolo Oss Mazzurana during the four podestarili periods comprised between 1872 and his death appears always supported from sturdy cultural and national ideals but also from solid economic bases, understandings to giving force to the demands for autonomy of the Trentino from the German Tyrol. The introduction of the electric power in the houses of Trento, the "democratic light", as he had defined, created workplaces and promoted the well-being of the popular classes, giving impulse to industrialization. At the same time Mazzurana promoted a series of studies in order to create an electrical tramway net, in order to permit workers to reach Trento from the surrounding area. Amongst the most important realizations are the new urban planning of the city, the new School Palace (currently School of Sociology), the renovation of the area of the railway station, the Kindergarten, and the new quarters opened for the labourers.

During the period of "economic renaissance" brought by Oss Mazzurana, Trento and Trentino can be aligned to the rest of Europe in the social and economic life, as well as in the cultural level.

Lineage

The Oss Mazzurana Family was known to be in various high-level public positions. Paolo fathered one son, Felice, who later became a renowned statesman and secretary of state to the provincial army. Felice eventually married and had three children: Maria, Rosa, and Giulio. Giulio, the eldest, inherited the 'Madruzzo' Villa (now considered an Italian Monument Heritage), and several rare Italian art pieces including works by Caravaggio and Botticelli. As a result of the ensuing threat of communism he sold the majority of his estate and escaped with his wife, Margherita Benvenuti, to Canada. The couple settled in Montreal, Quebec and had only one daughter, Bianca Oss Mazzurana, who became Bianca Ubaldini on marriage. Bianca was the sole remaining heir to the Oss Mazzurana name and enjoyed the afforded life style granted to her. Later in life, she married Arthur Ubaldini, Italian heir to the Ubaldini Distillery located in Trieste (Friuli-Venezia-Giulia). They divorced in 1982. Arthur and Bianca produced two children, Alberto (who ldied as a child of pneumonia), and Patrizia. Patrizia was extremely gifted in mathematics and at the age of 19 received a full-time scholarship to Loyola College University. It was during her formative years at Loyola where she met and fell in love with an older Loyola teaching assistant named Sergio Da Fre. Soon the coupled married, and within the ensuing ten years had their first child: Giulio Da Fre, in 1982. In 1984, Margueritta Maria Da Fre was born. In 1998, faced with the resulting economic downturn in the Quebec-Montreal regional urban economy, the couple, with their daughter Margueritta moved to Toronto. Sergio began to work as a notable Senior Marketing Specialist at the Bank of Montreal (Toronto Headquarters) and Patrizia (Patiricia, as spelled sometimes) continued to work as Project Manager also at the Bank of Montreal. Giulio had received a scholarship to attend the Ryerson Theatre School, however, wishing to live in a more so-called 'European Atmosphere' Giulio quickly left and moved to Montreal. He has since graduated with honours in philosophy at Concordia University, and has worked provisionally with the United Nations secretariat, department of the environment. Margueritta completed her European Studies degree at the University of Toronto in June 2006. She works as a technical analyst for Standard Life Insurance.

On the morning of September 8, 2006 Bianca Oss Mazzurana passed died at her residence Henri-Bradet in N.D.G., Montreal, Quebec, Canada.

Source (edited): "http://en.wikipedia.org/wiki/Paolo_Oss_Mazzurana"

Renzo Cramerotti

Renzo Cramerotti (born December 9, 1947 in Trento) is a retired male javelin thrower from Italy, who finished in 20th place at the 1972 Summer Olympics in Munich, West Germany. He set his personal best (83.50 metres) in 1971.

Source (edited): "http://en.wikipedia.org/wiki/Renzo_Cramerotti"

Roberto Sighel

Roberto Sighel (born 17 February 1967 in Trento) is a former Italian speedskater, with particularly strong achievements in the allround samalogue competitions. His skating career was unusually long, competing at top international level from 1988 to 2002. He participated in each of the 1988, 1992, 1994, 1998, 2002 Olympics, with 7th place his best result (10,000-m 1988, 5000-m 2002).

Sighel won the 1992 World Allround Championships, where he set a world record with 157.150 (37.38, 6:43,91, 1:52,38, 13:58,39). He also held the world record for *one hour skating*, with 41.041 km (26 mi), skated in Calgary 24 March 1999; this record lasted until Henk Angenent skated 41.669 km (26 mi) on 12 March 2004, also in Calgary.

In the World Allround Championships series, his results were 23 (1987), 6 (1988), 15 (1989), 2 (1991), 1 (1992), 6 (1993), 13 (1994), 3 (1995), 13 (1996), 22 (1997), 3 (1998), 4 (1999), 19 (2001), 7 (2002). His personal bests are 36.93 (500-m), 1:12.92 (1000-m), 1:47.47 (1500-m), 3:46.80 (3000-m), 6:25.11 (5000-m), 13:26.19 (10000-m).

Very few skaters manage to stay within the top ten of the Adelskalender over several seasons. Sighel is among those few, as he was no. 14 after the 1989 season, no. 15 after 1990, no. 9 after 1991, no. 2 after 1992, no. 3 after 1993, no. 4 after 1994, no. 4 after 1995, no. 5 after 1996, no. 7 after 1997, no. 3 after 1998, no. 3 after 1999, no. 5 after 2000, no. 13 after 2001, and no. 10 at career finish at 2002.

Source (edited): "http://en.wikipedia.org/wiki/Roberto_Sighel"

Rody Mirri

Rody Mirri

Rody Mirri, (Born 15 December 1952 in Trento, Italy) is a business manager, Italian author and TV producer.

Controversy

Striscia la Notizia an Italian satyrical TV programme has recently broadcasted images of Rody Mirry (taken by an hidden camera) making express sexual abuses on a underage potential actress. Many Italian female artists, allegedly discovered by Mr. Mirri and his so called scouting agency, have declared not to know him at all or say whether Mr. Mirri has sexually abused them (as Michelle Hunziker declared on Stiscia la Notizia - 10 March 2010).

TV Production & Shows

- LA CANZONE DEL CUORE (TMC, 1996)
- UN'ITALIANA PER MISS MONDO (ITALIA 7, 1997)
- OFF MUSIC (ODEON TV, 1998)
- RED & PASSION 2007 (DVD, 2007)
- IT'S YOUR SONG 2007 (NUMBERONE CHANNEL SKY, 2007)
- LA NOTTE DELLE STELLE (Bibione 1988, Desenzano del Garda 2002)
- ESTATE INSIEME (Italian Squares 1987)
- MISS LADY GOLF (Brescia 2002, Pinzolo 2002)
- DISCO MEETING (Bolzano Palaghiaccio 1976)
- MOTOR FASHION (Cervia 1987, Milano 2003)
- PREMIO NAZIONALE TRACCE (Lonato c/o Dehor 2002)
- ODEON UNO SPETTACOLO PER LA VITA (Milano Palatrussardi 1987)
- GRAN GALA UNICEF (Genova Costa Crociere 1988)
- LA DONNA DEL LAGO (Meet&Greet: Milano Grand Hotel Diana Majestic, Rimini Discoteca Paradiso, Iseo Piazza Garibaldi 2004)
- ESTATE VIP VARIETA' (San Teodoro Sardegna 1989, Manerba d/G 2005)
- RED&PASSION (Pesaro Adriatic Arena 2007)
- GRAN GALA IT'S YOUR SONG 2007 (Milano Executive Lounge, Brescia Mia Club, Riccione Hakuna Matata, Bastia Umbra The Barr 2007)
- GRAN GALA CROCE ROSSA ITALIANA (Milano Palatrussardi 1988)
- GRAN GALA DELLA MODA (Rimini 2007)
- NON VOLEVO FINISSE COSI' (Meet&Greet: Sarnico Cafè Imperial 2004)

Videoclip

- RED & PASSION (Dj Tiesto, 2007)

Source (edited): "http://en.wikipedia.org/wiki/Rody_Mirri"

Cognola

Cognola is a town in the province of Trento, Italy. Administratively it counts as one of the *frazioni* of the comune of Trento.

It has a population of c. 5,000 inhabitants.

Source (edited): "http://en.wikipedia.org/wiki/Cognola"

Mattarello

Location of the province of Trento

Mattarello is a small town in the province of Trento, Italy. It has been subsumed into a *frazione* of the *comune* of Trento, having previously been an independent *comune*. It has a population of 5,406. In the past it was a comune but the fascism delated it because of the wanted to do a "The big Trento" ("La grande Trento").

In Mattarello you can found the interdipartimental research centre CIBIO(Centre for Integrative Biology, part of University of Trento). The Centre will pursue the task of creating a suitable environment for merging classical cellular and molecular biology approaches with the new powerful tools of systems and synthetic biology, and with the contribution of chemistry, physics, informatics, mathematics, and engineering in an integrative view of basic biological processes and of their derangement in disease.

Trento airport is near the town, and there is an aeronautical museum, in the honour of Gianni Caproni.

Mattarello is also a Tuscan rolling pin Source (edited): "http://en.wikipedia.org/wiki/Mattarello"

Trento

Trento listen (traditional English: *Trent*; Italian: *Trento*, pronounced [ˈtrɛnto] or [ˈtrento]; local language: *Trènt*; German: *Trient*) is an Italian city located in the Adige River valley in Trentino-Alto Adige/Südtirol. It is the capital of the region and of the Autonomous Province of Trento.

In the English-speaking world, the city is most notable as the location of the **Council of Trent**. Trento is a major educational, scientific, financial and political centre in Trentino Alto-Adige and Northern Italy in general. The University of Trento ranks highly out of Italy's top 30 colleges, coming 1st in the Italian Ministry of Education ranking, 1st in Engineering area according to Censis-La Repubblica ranking and 5th in the Il Sole 24 ore ranking of Italian universities, and amongst the 500 best in the world, coming 407th. The city contains a picturesque Medieval and Renaissance historic centre, with ancient buildings such as Trento Cathedral and the Castello del Buonconsiglio.

Modern-day Trento is a cosmopolitan city, with highly-developed and organized modern social services. The city often ranks extremely highly out of all 103 Italian cities for quality of life, standard of living, and business and job opportunities, coming 1st, 6th and 2nd respectively. Trento is also one of the nation's wealthiest and most prosperous, with its province being one of the richest in Italy, although poorer than its neighbours Lombardy and South Tyrol, with a GDP per capita of €29,500 and a GDP (nominal) of €14.878 billion.

Geography

The township of Trento is geographically very large and encompasses the town centre as well as many suburbs of extremely varied geographical and population conditions (from the industrial suburb of Gardolo, just north of the city, to tiny mountain hamlets on the Monte Bondone). Various distinctive suburbs still maintain their traditional identity of rural or mountain villages.

Trento lies in a wide glacial valley called the Adige valley just south of the Alps foothill range Dolomite Mountains, where the Fersina and Avisio rivers join the Adige River (the second longest river in Italy). The Adige is one of the three main south-flowing Alpine rivers; its broadly curving course alongside Trento was straightened in 1850. The valley is surrounded by mountains, including the Vigolana (2,150 m), the Monte Bondone (2,181 m), the Paganella (2,124 m), the Marzola (1,747 m) and the Monte Calisio (1,096 m). Nearby lakes include the Lago di Caldonazzo, Lago di Levico, Lago di Garda and Lago di Toblino.

History

The origins of this city on the river track to Bolzano and the low Alpine passes of Brenner and the Passo di Resia (Reschenpass) over the Alps are disputed. Some scholars maintain it was a Rhaetian settlement: the Adige area was however influenced by neighbouring populations, including the (Adriatic) Veneti, the Etruscans, the Cimbri, and the Gauls (a Celtic people). According to other theories, the latter did instead found the city during the fourth century BC.

Trento was conquered by the Romans in the late 1st century BC, after several clashes with the Rhaetian tribes. The Romans gave their settlement the name *Tridentum* (Tri Dentum, meaning 'Three Teeth') because of the three hills that surround the city: the *Doss Trent*, *Sant'Agata* and *San Rocco*. The Latin name is the source of the adjective Tridentine. On the old townhall a Latin inscription is still visible: *Montes argentum mihi dant nomenque Tridentum* ("Mountains give me silver and the name of Trento"), attributed to Fra' Bartolomeo da Trento (died in 1251). Tridentum became an important stop on the Roman road that led from Verona to Innsbruck.

After the fall of the Western Roman Empire, the independent bishopric of Trento was ruled by Ostrogoths, Byzantines, Lombards and Franks, finally becoming part of the Holy Roman Empire. In 1027, Emperor Conrad II created the Prince-Bishops of Trento, who wielded both temporal and religious powers. In the following centuries, however, the sovereignty was divided between the Bishopric of Trent and the County of Tyrol (from 1363 part of the Habsburg monarchy). Around 1200, Trento became a mining center of some significance: silver was mined from the Monte Calisio - Khalisperg, and Prince-Bishop Federico Wanga issued the first mining code of the alpine region.

A dark episode in the history of Trento was the Trent blood libel. When a three year old Christian boy, Simonino, later known as Simon of Trent, disappeared in 1475 on the eve of Good Friday, the city's small Jewish community was accused of killing him and draining his blood for Jewish ritual purposes. Eight Jews were tortured and burned at the stake, and their families forced to convert to Christianity. The bishop of Trent, Johannes Hinderbach, had Simonino canonized and published the first book printed in Trent, "Story of a Christian Child Murdered at Trent," embellished with 12 woodcuts.

18th century copy of a late 16th-century map of Trento, northeast at top, showing walled old city and original course of the Adige.

In the 16th century Trento became notable for the Council of Trent (1545–1563) which gave rise to the Counter-Reformation. The adjective *Tridentine* (as in "Tridentine Mass") literally means pertaining to Trento, but can also refer to that specific event. Among the notable prince bishops of this time were Bernardo Clesio (who ruled the city 1514-1539, and managed to steer the Council to Trento) and Cristoforo Madruzzo (who ruled in 1539-1567), both able European politicians and Renaissance humanists, who greatly expanded and embellished the city.

During this period, and as an expression of this Humanism, Trento was also known as the site of a Jewish printing press. In 1558 Cardinal Madruzzo granted the privilege of printing Hebrew books to Joseph Ottolengo, a German rabbi. The actual printer was Jacob Marcaria, a local physician; after his death in 1562 the activity of the press of Riva di Trento ceased. Altogether thirty-four works were published in the period 1558 to 1562, most of them bearing the coat of arms of Madruzzo.

Prince-bishops ruled Trento until the Napoleonic era, when it bounced around among various states. Under the reorganization of the Holy Roman Empire in 1802, the Bishopric was secularized and annexed to the Habsburg territories. The Treaty of Pressburg in 1805 ceded Trent to Bavaria, and the Treaty of Schönbrunn four years later gave it to Napoleon's Kingdom of Italy. With Napoleon's defeat in 1814, Trento was finally annexed by the Habsburg Empire, becoming part of the province of Tyrol.

In the next decades Trento experienced a modernization of administration and economy with the first railroad in the Adige valley opening in 1859. During the late 19th century, Trento and Trieste, cities with ethnic Italian majorities still belonging to the Austrians, became icons of the Italian irredentist movement. Benito Mussolini briefly joined the staff of a local newspaper in 1908. The nationalist cause led Italy into World War I. Damiano Chiesa and Cesare Battisti were two well-known local irredentists who had joined the Italian army to fight against Austria-Hungary with the aim of bringing the territory of Trento into the new Kingdom of Italy. The two men were taken prisoners at the nearby southern front. They were put on trial for high treason and executed in the courtyard of Castello del Buonconsiglio (Cesare Battisti had served in the Austrian army). Their death caused an emotional outcry and was later used by the Italian government to celebrate the "liberation of Trento." The region was greatly affected during the war, and some of its fiercest battles were fought on the surrounding mountains.

After World War I, Trento and its Italian-speaking province, along with Bolzano (Bozen) and the part of Tyrol that stretched south of the Alpine watershed (which was, in the main, German speaking), were annexed by Italy.

In 1943, Mussolini was deposed and Italy surrendered to the Allies, who had invaded southern Italy via Sicily. German troops promptly invaded northern Italy and the provinces of Trento, Belluno and South Tyrol became part of the Operation Zone of the Alpine Foothills, annexed to Greater Germany. Some German-speakers wanted revenge upon Italians-speakers living in the area, but were mostly prevented by the occupying Nazis, who still considered Mussolini head of the Italian Social Republic and wanted to preserve good relations with the Fascists. From November, 1944 to April, 1945 Trento was bombed as part of the so-called "Battle of the

Brenner." War supplies from Germany to support the Gothic Line were for the most part routed through the rail line through the Brenner pass. Over 6,849 sorties were flown over targets from Verona to the Brenner Pass with 10,267 tons of bombs dropped. Parts of the city were hit by the Allied bombings, including the church of S. Maria Maggiore, the Church of the Annunciation and several bridges over the Adige river. In spite of the bombings, most of the medieval and renaissance town center was spared.

Starting from the 1950s the region has enjoyed prosperous growth, thanks in part to its special autonomy from the central Italian government.

Society and economy

Eight centuries of Prince-Bishop rulers, relative independence from the rest of Europe, the Austrian domination and a strong sense of communal fate left a distinctive mark on the city's culture, which is dominated by a fairly progressive Social-Catholic political orientation (in fact, Trento is one of the few cities in Italy where left-leaning Catholics form the majority party). The city is considered to be well-administered and enjoys the benefits of special autonomy from the central Italian government. Trento ranks high in Italian quality-of-life statistics.

The city owes much of its unique history to its position along the main communication route between Italy and Northern Europe and to the Adige river which prior to its diversion in the mid-19th century ran through the center of the city. The Adige river was formerly a navigable river and one of the main commercial routes in the Alps. The original course of the river is now covered by the Via Torre Vanga, Via Torre Verde and the Via Alessandro Manzoni.

University of Trento, Faculty of Science

As late as the Second World War, Trento depended on wine-making and silk. The manufacturing industry installed in the post-war period has been mostly dismantled. Today Trento thrives on commerce, services, tourism, high-quality agriculture and food industry (including wine, fruit), as a research and conference center thanks to a small but renowned university and research centers such as Fondazione Bruno Kessler, the Centre for Computational and Systems Biology and ECT*, and as logistics and transportation thoroughfare.

Valued pink and white porphyry is still excavated from some surrounding areas (Pila). This stone can be seen in many of Trento's buildings, both new and old.

The city has two long-running annual sporting events: the Giro al Sas (a 10 km professional road running competition) was first held in the city in 1907 and continues to the present, while the Giro del Trentino is an annual road cycling race which the city has hosted every year since 1963.

Politics

The administrative elections of May 3, 2009 were won by a Center-Left coalition. Results are the following (only parties with more than 4% are listed):
- Partito Democratico (Centre-left big tent party): 29.80%
- Unione per il Trentino (Centre-left Catholic party): 17.07%
- Popolo della Libertà (Center-Right): 11.92%
- Lega Nord (Northern Separatists): 7.78%
- Lista Civica Morandini (civic list supporting Morandini for mayor): 7.19%
- Trentino Tyrolean Autonomist Party (Autonomists): 4.72%

Current mayor is Alessandro Andreatta, of the Partito Democratico, elected with 64.42% of the votes.

Trento Cathedral.

Piazza Duomo, Case Rella frescoes.

Fountain of Neptune and *Torre Civica*.

Castello del Buonconsiglio.

Main sights

Although off the beaten path of mass tourism, Trento offers rather interesting monuments. Its architecture has a unique feel, with both Italian Renaissance and Germanic influences. The city center is small, and most Late-Medieval and Renaissance buildings have been restored to their original pastel colours and wooden balconies. Part of the medieval city walls is still visible in Piazza Fiera, along with a circular tower. Once, these walls encircled the whole town and were connected to the Castello del Buonconsiglio. The main monuments of the city include:

- *Duomo* (Cathedral of Saint Vigilius), a Romanesque-Gothic cathedral of the twelfth-thirteenth century, built on top of a late-Roman basilica (viewable in an underground crypt).
- *Piazza Duomo*, on the side of the Cathedral, with frescoed Renaissance buildings and the Late Baroque Fountain of Neptune (*Fontana di Nettuno*) built in 1767-1768.
- Church of *Santa Maria Maggiore* (1520), site of the preparatory congregations of the Third Council of Trent (April 1562 – December 1563). It was built for Bishop Bernardo Clesio by the architect Antonio Medaglia in Renaissance-Gothic style. The façade has a notable 16th century portal, while the interior has works by Giambettino Cignaroli and Moroni.
- *Castello del Buonconsiglio*, which includes a museum and the notable Torre dell'Aquila, with a cycle of fine Gothic frescoes depicting the months, commissioned by the prince-bishop Georg von Lichtenstein.
- Church of *San Pietro* (12th century) It has a neo-Gothic façade added in 1848-1850.
- Church of *Sant'Apollinare*, erected in the 13th century at the feet of the Doss Trento hill.
- Church of *San Lorenzo* (12th century). It has a notable Romanesque apse.
- *Torre Verde*, along the former transit path of the Adige river, is said to be where persons executed in the name of the Prince-Bishop were deposited in the river.
- *Palazzo delle Albere*, a Renaissance villa next to the Adige river built around 1550 by the Madruzzo family, now hosting a modern art museum.
- *Palazzo Pretorio*, next to the Duomo, of the 12th century, with a bell tower (*Torre Civica*) of the thirteenth century (it now hosts a collection of baroque paintings of religious themes). It was the main Bishops' residence until the mid-13th century.
- *Palazzo Salvadori* (1515).
- *Palazzo Geremia* (late 15th century). It has a Renaissance exterior and Gothic interiors.
- *Palazzo Lodron*, built during the Council of Trent. The interior has a large fresco cycle.
- Various underground remains of the streets and villas of the Roman city (in Via Prepositura and Piazza Cesare Battisti).

Trento also sports noteworthy modernist architecture, including the train station and the central post office, both by rationalist architect Angiolo Mazzoni. In particular, the train station (1934–36) is considered a landmark building of Italian railways architecture and combines many varieties of local stone with the most advanced building materials of the time: glass, reinforced concrete, metal. The post office was once decorated with colored windows by Fortunato Depero, but these were destroyed during bombings in World War II. Other buildings of that time include the Grand Hotel (by G. Lorenzi) with some guest rooms furnished with futurist furniture by Depero, and the "R. Sanzio" Primary School built by Adalberto Libera in 1931–34.

An important museum of modern art (Museo d'Arte di Trento e Rovereto) is located in the nearby town of Rovereto.

A notable aeronautical museum (Museo dell'Aeronautica Gianni Caproni) is located in Trento - Mattarello's Airport.

The Museo tridentino di scienze naturali (Trent Museum of Nature), is a museum of natural history and science.

Trento's surroundings are known for the beautiful mountain landscapes, and are the destination of both summer and winter tourism. The Alpine Botanical Garden, located on Monte Bondone in *Le Viotte* was founded in 1938 and is therefore probably the first such garden in Italy.

Trento is also the venue of a popular Mountain Film Festival

Notable natives

Alcide De Gasperi Memorial Monument.

In addition to the aforementioned Bernardo Clesio and Cristoforo Madruzzo, Giacomo Aconzio was born in Trento. Kurt von Schuschnigg was born in Riva del Garda, in the Trentino region. Other notable natives of Trento include:

- Beniamino Andreatta, politician.
- Lorenzo Bernardi, volleyball player

for the Italian national team who was declared "Player of the century" by an international jury.
- Francesco Antonio Bonporti, composer.
- Gianni Caproni, aeronautical engineer, born in Massone d'Arco 1886. Trento's airport is dedicated to him.
- Eusebio Chini, Jesuit Priest, missionary and explorer.
- Fortunato Depero, futurist artist and one of the founders of the futurist movement in Italy, was born in Fondo in 1892, close to Trento. He was later "adopted" by the city of Rovereto.
- Alcide De Gasperi, politician in Austria-Hungary, political leader and post-war premier in Italy and one of the founding fathers of the European Union, was born in Pieve Tesino, in the province of Trento.
- Felice Fontana, scientist.
- Gregorio Fontana, mathematician.
- Ernst von Koerber, prominent politician of the Austro-Hungarian Empire.
- Chiara Lubich, founder of the Focolare Movement.
- Gianfrancesco Malfatti, mathematician.
- Martino Martini, geographer, historian, missionary.
- Luigi Negrelli, engineer.
- Paolo Oss Mazzurana, Trento's most notable mayor. His tenure is characterized by progressive economic policies that impacted Trento's commercial sector and its eventual independence.
- Francesco Moser, cyclist
- Antonio Pedrotti, conductor and composer
- Andrea Pozzo, Jesuit Brother, baroque painter and architect.
- Giovanni Prati, poet and politician.
- Antonio Rosmini, priest, philosopher, born in Rovereto, 1797.
- Giovanni Antonio Scopoli, naturalist and physician, born in Cavalese.
- Giovanni Segantini, Italian Art Nouveau painter, was born in Arco in 1858.
- Alessandro Vittoria, mannerist sculptor.
- Riccardo Zandonai, opera composer.
- Francesca Neri, Award Winning Actress.
- Hermann Zingerle, neuropathologist

Transport

Highway A22-E45 links Trento with Verona and to Bolzano, Innsbruck and Munich.

Trento railway station, opened in 1859, forms part of the Brenner railway (Verona–Innsbruck), which is the main rail connection between Italy and Germany. The station is also a junction with the Valsugana railway, which connects Trento with Venice. Trento has several other railway stations, including Trento FTM, terminus of the Trento-Malè-Marilleva railway (FTM).

Bus or train services operate to the main surrounding valleys: Fassa, Fiemme, Gudicarie, Non, Primiero, Rendena, Sole, Tesino, Valsugana.

The public transport network within the city consists of 20 bus lines operated by Trentino Trasporti and a funicular service to Sardagna. The various railway stations within Trento's city limits are integrated into the public transport network.

Demographics

In 2007, there were 112,637 people residing in Trento, of whom 48% were male and 52% were female. Minors (children ages 18 and younger) totalled 18.01 percent of the population compared to pensioners who number 19.37 percent. This compares with the Italian average of 18.06 percent (minors) and 19.94 percent (pensioners). The average age of Trento residents is 41 compared to the Italian average of 42. In the five years between 2002 and 2007, the population of Trento grew by 5.72 percent, while Italy as a whole grew by 3.56 percent. The current birth rate of Trento is 9.61 births per 1,000 inhabitants compared to the Italian average of 9.45 births.

As of 2006, 92.68% of the population was Italian. The largest immigrant group came from other European countries (mostly Albania, Romania): 4.13%, North Africa: 1.08%, and the Americas: 0.85%. The population consists of Roman Catholic and Protestant groups. Also, there is a modest indigenous German minority who are considered Italian.

International relations

Twin towns - Sister cities

Trento is twinned with:
Districts of Trento are twinned with

Partner cities

- Prijedor, Bosnia and Herzegovina
- Sławno, Poland

Frazioni

- Povo
- Villazzano
- Gardolo
- Roncafort
- Mattarello
- Martignano
- Cognola
- Ravina
- Romagnano
- Montevaccino
- Vela, Meano
- Sardagna
- Sopramonte
- Vigo Meano
- Gazzadina
- Candriai
- Vaneze
- Cadine
- Vigolo Baselga

Source (edited): "http://en.wikipedia.org/wiki/Trento"

Trento Calcio 1921

Trento Calcio 1921 (also nicknamed *i Gialloblu* or *gli Aquilotti*) is an Italian association football, and the major football club in Trento, Trentino-Alto Adige/Südtirol. It plays in Serie D. The official colours are yellow and blue.

The club took part to the 1945–46 Serie B-C Alta Italia season.
Source (edited): "http://en.wikipedia.org/wiki/Trento_Calcio_1921"

Trento railway station

Trento railway station (Italian: *Stazione di Trento*) serves the city and *comune* of Trento, capital of the autonomous region of Trentino-Alto Adige/Südtirol, northeastern Italy. Opened in 1859, it forms part of the Brenner railway (Verona–Innsbruck), and is also a junction with the Valsugana railway, which connects Trento with Venice.

The station is currently managed by Rete Ferroviaria Italiana (RFI). However, the commercial area of the passenger building is managed by Centostazioni. Train services to and from the station are operated by Trenitalia. Each of these companies is a subsidiary of Ferrovie dello Stato (FS), Italy's state-owned rail company.

Adjacent to the station is another station, the Trento terminus of the metre gauge Trento-Malè-Marilleva railway (FTM).

Location

Trento railway station is situated at Piazza Dante, at the northern edge of the city centre.

Features

The external colonnade.

The passenger building houses the ticket office and waiting room as well as other facilities such as a bar and a newsstand.

The station yard has four tracks equipped with platforms: the adjacent sidings are used mainly for trains traversing the Valsugana railway. The platforms are connected by both underpass and elevator.

There are also a locomotive shed and a turntable.

The goods yard is situated at Roncafort, a short distance to the north along the Brenner railway.

Passenger and train movements

The station has about 5.5 million passenger movements each year, and is therefore the second busiest in the region in terms of numbers of passengers, after Bolzano/Bozen.

All trains passing through Trento, including InterCity and Eurostar Italia trains, stop at the station. The main domestic destinations are Verona, Venezia, Bassano del Grappa and Bolzano/Bozen, but passengers also depart for and arrive from other domestic destinations such as Bologna or Rome. The main international links are with Munich and Innsbruck.
Source (edited): "http://en.wikipedia.org/wiki/Trento_railway_station"

University of Trento

The **University of Trento** is an Italian university that was founded in 1962. It has been able to achieve considerable results in didactics, research and international relations, as shown by Censis University Guide (where the University of Trento regularly appears in the first five positions, both in the general and faculties ranking) and by the Italian Ministry of Education (according to which the University of Trento is the most virtuous university in Italy).

The didactic and scientific activities are concentrated around three main "areas": the "polo di città" (city area), with the Faculties of Economics, Sociology, Law, Arts and Humanities; the "polo collina" (hill area) with the Faculties of Mathematical, Physical and Life sciences and the Faculty of Engineering, the "polo di Rovereto" (Rovereto area) with the Faculty of Cognitive Sciences.

The University is among the promoters of the Festival dell'Economia of Trento (Festival of Economics).

History

The University of Trento was founded in 1962 as a Higher University Institute for Social Sciences. It then became the first Faculty of Sociology in Italy. The impact on the city was quite contradictory: the University was seen both as a motivating force for cultural openness and the creation of a new leading class, but also as a fracturing element of protest.

In order to expand the educational opportunities of the University of Trento, in 1972 the Faculty of Science was founded (with Engineering) and in 1973, so was the Faculty of Economics. The academic project was even more widened in 1984 with the Faculties of Arts and Humanities and Law and in 1985 with the Faculty of Engineering. In 2004 the Faculty of Cognitive Sciences was founded, as the first of its kind in Italy.

Internationalization

Special importance has been given to the International dimension of the University ever since its first years. The University has focused on the development of strategic international alliances in the view of complementarity. The

University has partnerships with prestigious universities and research centers all over the world and is part of important cooperation networks (for instance Consorzio Time, Asea-Uninet GE4).

Besides the LLP-Erasmus project, ever since 1997, the University has also supported double degree agreements. The most recent one is the double degree in Civil Engineering with the University of Tongi China (May 2008): students can achieve a Master in Civil Engineering and the two year Master course in Civil Engineering in Trento. The University is also part of the Erasmus Mundus programme and the Erasmus Mundus External cooperation window (now called action 2 of Erasmus Mundus II).

The University also has a number of bilateral agreements with universities in Asia, America, the Middle East and Oceania. There are also many collaborations for development co-operation, with African and Latin American universities. Foreign Tenured scholars and Visiting professors are 10% of the total amount of professors. The University is investing in calling high profile foreign scholars and different Italian scholars have arrived in Trento after important experiences abroad, contributing to the internationalization of the University. The collaboration with Germany brought Trento to being chosen as the Italian seat of the Italian-German University, an institution that deals with coordination for advanced training and research between Italian and German universities.

Acknowledgements

In 2012, the University of Trento will celebrate its first 50 years: a tradition that brings it to be acknowledged as one of the leading universities in Italy, as indicated by several national rankings: the university ranks in first position for the quality of its research and didactics in the MIUR ranking and in first place in the overall ranking in the 2010 Censis Guide from La Repubblica newspaper; in the annual ranking by the newspaper Il Sole 24 Ore, the university is in 5th place among Italian public universities.

In the QS World University ranking 2010, the University of Trento is one of the few Italian universities mentioned, confirming its placement in the 401–500 bracket, while charting in the 201–300 bracket in the Engineering, Natural Sciences and Social Sciences subject rankings.

The University of Trento is ranked 252nd overall (and 5th in Italy) in the Times Higher Education World University Rankings 2010.

Courses

Faculty of Economics
- Undergraduate courses
  - Business administration and law (L18)
  - Business management (L18)
  - Economics and Management (L18, L33)
- Master's courses (two-year duration)
  - Bank business and financial market (19/S)
  - Economic decision-making, business and social responsibility (64/S)
  - Environmental and tourism economics and management (83/S)
  - International management*1 (LM77)
  - Management and consulting* (LM77)
  - Net-Economy. Technology and management of information and knowledge (100/S)

Faculty of Law
- Five-year Master's course
  - Law

Faculty of Engineering
- Undergraduate courses
  - Civil engineering* (L7)
  - Electronics and telecommunications engineering (L8)
  - Environmental and land engineering* (L7)
  - Food industry engineering (L9)
  - Industrial engineering (L9)
  - Information and business organisation engineering (L8)

- Five-year Master's course:
  - Architectural engineering (4/S)
- Master's courses (two-year duration):
  - Civil engineering (LM23)
  - Environmental and land engineering (LM35)
  - materials engineering (LM22)
  - Mechatronics engineering (LM33)
  - Telecommunication engineering1 (LM27)

Faculty of Arts and Humanities
- Undergraduate courses
  - Cultural heritage (L1)
  - Historical, philological and literary studies (L10)
  - Modern languages* (L11, L12)
  - Philosophy (L5)
- Master's courses (two-year duration):
  - Cultural heritage: preservation and management (LM89, LM2)
  - Euroamerican literatures, translation and literary criticism (LM37)
  - Historical sciences and forms of memory (LM84, LM5)
  - Language mediation, tourism and cultures* (LM49)
  - Philology and literary criticism (LM14)
  - Philosophy and the languages of modernity (LM78)

Faculty of Cognitive Sciences
- Undergraduate courses
  - Interfaces and communication technology (L20)
  - Professional health educator * – in collaboration with the University of Ferrara (2/SNT)
  - Sciences and techniques of cognitive psychology (L24)
- Master's courses (two-year duration)
  - Cognitive Science*1 (LM55)
  - Psychology (LM51)

Faculty of Mathematical, Physical and Natural Science
- Undergraduate courses
  - Biomolecular sciences and technologies* (L2)
  - Computer science (L31)

- Mathematics (L35)
- Physics (L30)
- Master's courses (two-year duration)
  - Computer science1 (LM18)
    - Graduate Program in Information Science and Technology
  - Mathematics (LM40)
  - Physics (LM17)
- Master's courses (one-year duration)
  - Master in Technologies for eGovernment

Graduate schools

School of International Studies

- Master's courses (two-year duration)
  - European and international studies – course with admission test (LM52)
- Master's course (one year duration)
  - Peace Building and Conflict Resolution

School on Local Development

- Master's course (one year duration)
  - Joint European Master in Comparative Local Development

Research departments

- Economics
- Philosophy, History and Cultural heritage
- Physics
- Computer and management sciences
- Information Engineering and Computer Science
- Civil and Environmental Engineering
- Materials Engineering and Industrial Technologies
- Mechanical and Structural Engineering
- Mathematics
- Cognitive and education sciences
- Juridical sciences
- Human and social sciences
- Sociology and social research
- Literary, language and philological studies

Services

Services dealing with the right to study are the University's flagship. Aspects like the receptiveness of the Faculties, the canteens, accommodation, study areas and the library are important moments for students' lives and the University keeps investing for this. In collaboration with the Opera Universitaria, the University offers 1500 accommodations in the San Bartolomeo Campus, in student residences or flats that have special agreements with the University. The University has a central library composed of different buildings (in each Faculty) where students can consult books or borrow them, study or use the internet, with long opening hours (even until midnight), open Saturday and Sunday.

With the Welcome Office, the University supports International students and researchers in the administrative procedures connected with their arrival and stay in Trento (entry visa, residence permit, health insurance, accommodation, National insurance number, etc) and gives information as regards the modalities and documentation needed to enroll. The office also organizes social events and trips: Welcoming day, sessions dedicated to the spread of information, excursions and socio-cultural activities to help guests integrate in the University and territory.

The contributions and aid for fee payment are a relevant issue for the University. Thanks to the Opera Universitaria, the University is able to offer students grants. Starting from academic year 2008/2009, the University radically changed its university fees system, emphasizing merit and students' efforts. Those who enroll have the chance to apply for grants up to € 4.000.

The latest project born at the University of Trento is UNI.sport, the new university network for sports services and facilities dedicated to the students of the University of Trento.

Deans

- 1962 – 1968 Mario Volpato
- 1968 – 1970 Francesco Alberoni
- 1970 Norberto Bobbio
- 1970 – 1972 Guido Baglioni
- 1972 – 1978 Paolo Prodi
- 1977 – 1978 Ezio Clementel
- 1978 – 1990 Fabio Ferrari
- 1990 – 1996 Fulvio Zuelli
- 1996 – 2004 Massimo Egidi
- 2004 – today Davide Bassi

Honorary professors

- Imrich Chlamtac
- Jean-Paul Fitoussi
- Mikhail Gorbačëv, ex President of the Soviet Union.
- Tenzin Gyatso, born Lhamo Dondrub, XIV Dalai Lama.
- Václav Klaus, President of the Czech Republic
- James March
- Giorgio Napolitano, President of the Italian Republic, awarded on 11 February 2008

Source (edited): "http://en.wikipedia.org/wiki/University_of_Trento"